Bridging
the
Generations

Bridging the Generations

Katie Funk Wiebe

Foreword by Sara Wenger Shenk

Herald
Press

Scottdale, Pennsylvania
Waterloo, Ontario

Library of Congress Cataloging-in-Publication Data
Wiebe, Katie Funk.
    Bridging the generations / Katie Funk Wiebe ; foreword by Sara
Wenger Shenk.
        p. cm.
    Includes bibliographical references.
    ISBN 0-8361-9162-5 (pbk. : alk. paper)
        1. Intergenerational relations—Religious aspects—Christianity.
2. Christian aged—Religious life. 3. Church. I. Title.

BV640 . W59 2001
261.8'342—dc21

                                                        2001024366

The paper used in this publication is recycled and meets the minimum
requirements of American National Standard for Information Sciences—
Permanence of Paper for Printed Library Materials, ANSI Z39.48-1984.

Scripture is used by permission, with all rights reserved, and unless otherwise
noted, is from the NIV, from *The Holy Bible, New International Version*, copyright ®, copyright © 1973, 1978, 1984 by International Bible Society,
Zondervan Publishing House.

BRIDGING THE GENERATIONS
Copyright © 2001 by Herald Press, Scottdale, Pa. 15683
        Published simultaneously in Canada by Herald Press,
        Waterloo, Ont. N2L 6H7. All rights reserved
Library of Congress Catalog Card Number: 2001024366
International Standard Book Number: 0-8361-9162-5
Printed in the United States of America
Book and cover design by Jim Butti
Cover photo by Skjold Photographs

10 09 08 07 06 05 04 03 02 01 10 9 8 7 6 5 4 3 2 1

To order or request information, please call 1-800-759-4447 (individuals); 1-800-245-7894 (trade). Website: www.mph.org

Dedicated to the memory of
Christine
My faithful supporter

Contents

Foreword

This is an I-have-a-dream kind of book—a book that envisions the recovery of true, intergenerational community. Katie Funk Wiebe invites us to dream with her even as she elaborates on the patterns of age segregation that undermine the networking essential to our well-being. Her passionate prose stirs us toward imagining a world of generations reuniting for the mutual blessing of all.

As an elder herself, Wiebe speaks like one intimately acquainted from the inside with the pain of alienation that too often insinuates itself into our relationships. She speaks on behalf of those who experience the prejudice of "ageism" first hand. As an articulate advocate for her "own people" she objects to the unfair labels that shove all people over retirement age into one broad category. Yet Wiebe also speaks out on behalf of youth who are frequently and summarily dismissed as "irresponsible" teenagers. Lumping people together into age categories—and other categories as well—negates their uniqueness and has a devastating effect on the health and well-being of our communities.

A strain of lament weaves itself into these pages, a lament for the loss of connectedness, the loss of esteem for elders as sages, prophets, keepers of memory, and conveyors of wisdom. Wiebe reminds us of the intergenerational connections that have normally characterized human experience over the centuries and examines some possible explanations for our current age-constricted subcultures. And there is pathos to the lament as it becomes apparent that the lack of human connections includes not only misguided stereotyping, but also a discounting of wisdom itself as a necessary ingredient of life. Few seem to be listening for wisdom. There is little demand for wisdom. The information age so inundates us with superfluous, fragmented knowledge that we lose sight of what it means to live artfully, gracefully, wisely.

But Wiebe is our seer, our prophetic guide. With a sturdy hold on faith, and a clear-sighted vision, she shows us once again what is required for true human flourishing through the recovery of intergenerational connections. She does this not by elaborating on a whole new set of church programs, but by guiding us toward imagining new and revived relationships.

What she calls us to is not hard work, or expensive new initiatives, or even anything very risky or heroic. She calls us simply to see our communities in new ways—not as multilayered, segmented organizations, but as organisms that for their health and well-being must be integrally and vitally reconnected. The lifeblood of our communities must flow freely throughout the whole body so the whole can be nourished by all of its interconnecting parts. When we grasp a vision of wholeness whose dynamism is dependent on the reconnecting of all parts, our resolve to bring the generations together will be quickened.

The vision for reconnection then will lead us toward new patterns. Rather than studying the Bible in age segregated groupings, why don't we learn to study it together again? Rather than working at disaster relief or neighborhood service projects with our peers only, why not see these opportunities as prime time to teach and learn new skills from others older or younger than ourselves. Rather than sharing our stories only with our peers, why not look for intergenerational settings for storytelling.

We begin by asking ourselves some basic questions. Where can we hear each other's stories? Who are the heroes among us? Have we paid attention to the ordinary acts of heroism that characterize the lives of every one of our elders? How can we create the opportunities in our worship/fellowship/educational events for their stories of loss and suffering, of hurt and forgiveness, of betrayal and faithfulness to be shared?

What are we doing to empower elders to recognize what they have that would be of value to others? How are we equipping them to become encouragers, cheerleaders of the youth? Who nurtures mentoring relationships that build partnering connections between elders and youth? How do we encourage youth to seek out elders and learn from them?

These are questions that inform the vision that Wiebe sketches for us. She not only dreams big dreams. She also offers many practical suggestions for rebuilding damaged connections. Her dream is laced with illustrations that tug at the heart. Her dream is made concrete with many pointers that make reconnecting look doable.

Wiebe's dream is compelling because it seems so touchable, so attainable, even as it eludes us. In order for it to become real among us, we need first to stop and lament what has been lost. For many the quality of our human connections with family, grandparents, friends, youth, and elders has deteriorated. Many of us, without noticing, are rushing pell-mell toward anonymity and worse.

Now, with Wiebe's prophetic beckoning we are offered a chance to stop and pay attention. We're invited to reclaim what has been lost. We're guided in envisioning ways to rebuild the connections on which our lives depend. We are given the opportunity to choose once again to spend time with each other, listening—listening for some wise person to say when we are unnerved by the treacherous water, "I've felt the bottom and it is firm."

Wiebe has offered us a book firmly grounded in intergenerational wisdom and the unfailing love of God. Her book moves us toward renewing the life-giving bonds between generations so that we will all recognize the ageless image of God in each other.

—*Sara Wenger Shenk*
Harrisonburg, Virginia
January 2001

Preface

This book was born out of a concern that all generations in the congregation belong together. It does not purport to be the whole answer. It is a probing of the issue and the beginning of an answer to a question being asked in both secular and religious worlds: Have age-groups strayed too far apart in the last half century? Is there hope for bringing them closer together again?

As the family enters the church, each person heads in a different direction. It is an unquestioned practice. Infants and toddlers are carried to the nursery. The main body of adults migrates to the sanctuary. At the appropriate moment the young children leave the worship service for their own gathering geared to their level of understanding. Sometimes youth worship in a different style in separate gatherings. Even adult Sunday school classes are often age-segregated. The result is a multilayered church, in which each layer remains distinct.

This book is about the gaps between the generations—any generation—but primarily about the gap between young and old. Today we encourage the young to believe, and to be baptized, and we should, but their serious sustained interaction with adults, as young adults, is often limited. As baptized members they are not really expected to take on adult believer responsibilities. At the same time the music, movies, television programming, and other aspects of our teenage culture encourage them more and more to indulge in adolescent behavior, as if it were their right. An underlying assumption in our church culture is that teenagers, even those who call themselves Christians, must first be allowed to mature physically, mentally, and spiritually before they can join the actual body of Christ.

The other group pertinent to this discussion of reconnecting the generations is rapidly increasing in number in our congregations. They are our elders. I use the term deliberately. We are more comfortable with euphemisms like "seniors" and sometimes even "golden-agers." In some congregations elders is a term for a body of wise people in the church who oversee spiritual life.

Psychiatrist Allen B. Chinen in *The Ever After: Fairy Tales and the Second Half of Life* says traditional cultures make the distinction between elders and elderly. An elder is growing and developing and sees the positive opportunities in the second half of life. The elderly become depressed and despairing. According to Zalman Schachter-Shalomi and Ronald S. Miller in *From AGE-ing to SAGE-ing*, elders have a positive self-identity and become sages and have wisdom to offer their families and communities. The elderly have a sense of isolation, loneliness, and lack positive social roles.

Whatever we may call this group of older adults, they are living longer. According to a paper prepared for the United Nations sponsored International Year of Older Persons (1999) by the American Association of Retired Persons, persons 60 years and older constitute an ever-increasing proportion of the world population. Persons 85 and older are the fastest growing age-group in most parts of the world. Population aging is occurring most rapidly in developing nations, countries that, in many cases, are the least equipped to respond to the challenges posed by this phenomenon.

In 1996 the 65-74 age-group in the United States was

eight times larger than in 1900, but the 75-84 group was 16 times larger and the 85+ group was 31 times larger. By 2030, there will be about 70 million older persons, more than twice their number in 1996. People 65 and over represented 13 percent of the population in the year 2000, but will be 20 percent by 2030.* In the church, this figure is often increased by at least 10 to 12 percent because church membership and attendance is an important aspect of their lives.

The "young" elders are usually still vigorous, have much to offer, but are still being set aside or pushed to the fringes of church life. Sometimes they choose that direction themselves. In family life grandparents are often far removed from children and grandchildren. Elders without close relatives are still further removed from children in general. The frail elderly are shunted off to various kinds of housing arrangements where they won't interfere with their children's lives. Someone has spoken of this splitting of the foundation of our spiritual family a mockery of God's plan for the body of Christ. But that is changing.

Whenever a new need arises in the body of Christ, the church has worked to alleviate that need. This pattern began with the early church in Acts, which was growing faster than the leaders could identify and address the problems. The Grecian Jews complained against the Aramaic-speaking Christians because their widows were not getting enough in the daily distribution of food.

The complaint didn't last long. The twelve apostles immediately agreed there was a problem and did something about it. Seven deacons "full of the Spirit and wisdom" were selected to work with this need. No widow, regardless of her ethnic background, should suffer in the emerging church of Jesus Christ. They recognized that the church had spiritually gifted people able to take care of this lack.

How does one change the emphasis of a congregation from a multilayered approach to greater integration? First, one needs to be convinced there is a lack in the same way the early apostles recognized the needs of the widows. That awareness comes about today by reading, observing, praying, working, and, yes, I'll say it, by skillful use of the Internet: Not first by changing structures.

This book is not about electing new committees and appointing study commissions or adding heavy administrative loads to already overburdened "bureaucrats" with the hope of introducing extensive new intergenerational life into the church.

This is a book about changing attitudes, about intergenerational relationships in the church—and about bringing all generations closer together. It is about listening to the voice of God urging us to stretch out and touch one another, whatever the age, to make peoplehood a reality. This is a book about changing a culture of age segregation to a culture of connectedness.

The focus of this book will primarily be on connecting elders and youth rather than on bringing together middle adults and their parents or the younger generations. To try to deal with all generation gaps would have meant a much larger volume. This book is written from my perspective as an older adult reflecting about what I see happening, or not happening, as I consider what society has done to elders and what we have done to ourselves to keep the gap widening.

The message of this book is that elders can be enormously enriching to younger generations. It is not meant to be a book for professionals, but for anyone with even just a casual interest in the topic. So I have written it in conversational style, adding anecdotes from my own experience to keep you reading. I hope it will spark some good discussions.

A book like this has many roots. Though it officially began with a request by Byron Rempel-Burkholder of Faith & Life Press to consider writing a manuscript about the generation gap, thoughts related to this topic had harbored in my mind for several years.

At a conference on aging, I heard Elbert C. Cole, founder of the Shepherd's Centers of America, urge elders to take their place in church and society as encouragers of the young. I discussed with Dwight E. Roth of Hesston College his longtime concerns about the growing generation gap and his efforts to bridge it through his work at the college. He convinced me this was a needed topic to explore for today's church.

When I told friends what I was writing, they paused a moment, trying to grasp what I was saying, and then enthusiastically agreed it was an important subject. I thank them for their support.

I also appreciate the many writers and speakers who influenced my general thinking on the subject. To give each one credit is difficult.

I thank those people who allowed me to test my ideas on them in groups or individually to see if they were a good fit, not too loose, not too tight. I especially appreciate the support of Naomi Gaede Penner, Joyce Parker, and Dwight E. Roth who read the manuscript and offered valuable comments. I thank David E. Hostetler for his careful work as editor.

I acknowledge Kindred Press' permission to reprint several paragraphs from my book *Alone: A Search for Joy.*

A farm boy was told by his father to fetch the cows. Shortly thereafter the boy's sister asked him why he was climbing the windmill. "To fetch the cows," he replied.

"Up there?" she asked. He climbed the windmill to locate the cows. Join me at the top of the windmill to find better ways for the generations to connect.

—*Katie Funk Wiebe*
  Wichita, Kansas, October 2000

* *Statistics in this book are from* A Profile of Older Americans 1997 *published by the American Association of Retired Persons and refer only to the United States population unless otherwise stated. Some overseas third-world countries have much lower life expectancy and the number of older adults is therefore much smaller. But the general trend is for an aging population worldwide.*

Bridging the Generations

Chapter 1

God's Intention
for the Generations

*"Praise the Lord . . . young men and maidens, old men and
children. Let them praise the name of the Lord. . . ."*

I can trace my genealogy back to Prussia and the year
1769. My grandmother copied it from someone else's
copy. I copied it from her records.

As I read it I think of those early ancestors in a horse
and wagon moving slowly, day after day, with children
and other neighbors, some livestock and farming equipment, to their new home in the Ukraine in the late 18th
century. I also think of my grandmother and her life as a
miller's wife during the Russian Revolution.

This genealogy reminds me forcefully that I am part
of a people with a story, a much bigger story than just
my immediate family; and at times I feel compelled to
tell my children this larger story. And to say, "This is
who we are."

I'd start with the genealogies in Genesis. The
Israelites had a strong sense of their history as a people.
At important junctures in the life of the people, leaders
repeated the tales of Abraham, Isaac, and Jacob, who
had been led of God, and were now urging the Israelites
to see themselves as God's people. But they didn't tell
stories of isolated significant individuals in their past.
Quite the opposite. They told the stories of the patriarchs

to show that even they were part of the flow of history. Generation followed generation. Each generation influenced the next, sometimes for good, sometimes for evil. The flow never ceased.

African-American poet Langston Hughes, in his much published poem "The Negro Speaks of Rivers," writes how this flow relates to his people: "I've known rivers ancient as the world and older than the flow of human blood in human veins." His poem focuses on the Euphrates, the cradle of human life; the Congo and the Nile, where his people lived for centuries; and the Mississippi, where the story of the African-Americans continues. He is part of all these. He joins in a river-like fusion with his ancestors.

Genealogies are a river of life. I think of Hughes' poem whenever I read the genealogies of Genesis 5. They comprise a river of life that flows on and on in each succeeding generation. The repetitiveness and symmetry of the biblical accounts add to this sense of continuity. Like a "super-energizer bunny," the generations flow on uninterrupted. In James Michener's epic novel, *Hawaii,* unschooled native Hawaiians recite their lineage going back 80 generations to an earlier, primitive culture. This knowledge of their lineage, taught to each succeeding generation, brought a sense of identity and wholeness to their race. It revealed where they had originally come from, the dreams of their foreparents, their struggles and successes.

Genealogies are revealing. The line of Cain, the murderer of Abel, told in six generations (Gen. 4:16-24), is devoted to things earthy and apart from God. The story of the conflict between Cain and Abel was not an isolated event, but a link in a chain of events. The line of Seth,

Cain's brother (Gen. 4:25—5:32), told in ten generations, is also a record of living and dying, but of a people directed toward God. The story of Enoch who walked with God was not an isolated bright spot in a world of darkness, but shows how even then one generation affected the next. *The genealogies speak to a concept of the wholeness or interconnectedness of life.*

God had made a covenant with the Israelites, his chosen people. They belonged to him, not just as individuals, but as a people, generation after generation. The young Hebrew children were reminded of this at many celebrative occasions. No child heard this story as merely a historical account. They were told their story to show that God was involved in everything that happened and that their story was leading somewhere.

The psalmist in the storytelling psalms brought to his listeners' ears the trials in the wilderness, the famines, plagues, defeats in war, oppression, and release from slavery. He established solidarity with generations that had gone before. His writings revealed God's loving kindness and care for his people. The Sunday school teacher or minister who can relate the Bible story to events in individual and church life is the wise teacher.

A true community includes all generations. This is the significant point in this intergenerational study: No one can live a holy life alone. We are a community, a people of God. When children discover that they are members of a larger body, the church, as a well as the family, faith has a vast room full of things to show the child. For faith is something you see or experience with others. Many older adults learned what the Christian life was all about by enduring long, even boring, services, and listening in on heavy discussions of their elders about fellow members erring from the pathway, and stumbling toward God. These experiences subconsciously formed their theology. They learned the church was a community, a people of God, with common goals and a common identity.

A true community of God, according to Scripture, includes all generations, all ages of believers, not just adults. Former missionary John Driver, in *Becoming God's Community*, states that building community is the specific agenda of God's people. The first church in Acts began with a common life of sharing, healing, worshiping, and witnessing. Was it limited to only adults? Were young adults included? Teenagers, of course, were an unknown entity at that time. In biblical times you moved directly from childhood to adulthood. Young Hebrew boys were included in the adult family at the age of twelve.

When the apostle Peter came to Cornelius' house he found awaiting his message the kinsmen of Cornelius and near friends, and also his whole family (Acts 10:27-46).

The apostle Paul also preached to family groups who became converts of the Christian way. One was the household of Lydia, a businesswoman from the city of Thyratira, who sold purple dye in the city (Acts 16:14-15).

The second household to which Paul preached in Philippi was the jailer's. Paul and Silas preached not only to the jailer but "to all that were in his house," children, young people, and grown-ups, all who had been awakened by the earthquake.

Psalm 78 is a passage that also emphasizes the interrelatedness of the generations.

I will open my mouth in parables,
I will utter hidden things, things from of old—

what we have heard and known,
what our fathers have told us.
We will not hide them from their children;
we will tell the next generation
the praiseworthy deeds of the Lord,
his power, and the wonders he has done.
He decreed statutes for Jacob
and established the law in Israel,
which he commanded our forefathers
to teach their children,
so the next generation would know them,
even the children yet to be born
and they in turn would tell their children.
Then they would put their trust in God
and would not forget his deeds
but would keep his commands (Ps. 78:2-7).

The lesson in this psalm is that in God's economy no person is an isolated being, whether parent or child. He or she is a member of the people of God. The psalms, if studied as a body of literature, reveal that the poet has a strong hunger for a closer relationship to God, like a deer that thirsts for water (Ps. 42:1). But Bernard Anderson writes in *Out of the Depths* that this longing for a one-to-one relationship with God wasn't a case of going off into a corner to worship by oneself, in a kind of private piety or individual spiritual experience. The poet yearns to be involved in the believing and worshiping community, to participate in the worship services of the temple, and to celebrate with the people the presence of God in their midst.

No worshiper in isolation. You couldn't be an Israelite worshiper in isolation. You were always part of the worshiping community, one that didn't begin with that person's generation but with all the generations that preceded it. That was a given. But another given was that you could have a personal relationship with God even as you were a member of the community.

In the Old Testament, the prophet Joel calls together the people, including the elders, the children, the nursing mothers, the young bridegroom and his bride, the priests who minister to the people, to weep and plead before God for renewal (Joel 2:16-17).

As they sat with their parents, were the young aware of the urgency of the situation, that the destructive day of the Lord was approaching? Did they grasp that everyone, young and old, would receive a portion of the outpouring of the Spirit? (Joel 2:28-32). That everyone, young and old, men and women, would have a role in prophesying? And that the elders and young men had the special task of envisioning (dreaming about) the future?

No distinctions of age, sex, or class. In Acts, the apostle Peter, speaking to the masses, under the moving of the Spirit, quotes from the prophet Joel to show that the old distinctions of class, sex, and age have been erased. But then he makes a significant comment for this study on reconnecting the generations:

In the last days, God says,
I will pour out my Spirit on all people.
Your sons and daughters will prophesy,
your young men will see visions,
your old men will dream dreams.
Even on my servants, both men and women,
I will pour out my Spirit in those days,
and they will prophesy (Acts 2:17-18).

If you read this passage too fast, you will miss it as many of us have over the years. Peter includes young men and women, young and old men. Christian feminists, both men and women, have highlighted the phrase about daughters prophesying to strengthen their cause that they too have a gift from the Spirit to be used within the church. Was the inclusion of all generations, old and young, a new thought to the ancient Hebrews as much as including both genders as prophets is a new thought to our present church world?

The strong repetition, sons and daughters, young men and old men, seems to leave no doubt of God's intention to include, right from the beginning of the new church age, both male and female, old and young, and all social classes among his prophets or teaching servants.

Whereas in the Old Testament the Holy Spirit was given primarily to people with official positions in Israelite theocracy such as kings (David, Solomon), priests (Eli, Samuel), and prophets (Elijah, Elisha), now Peter was teaching that in this new era it would also be given to young and old, men and women, all classes, all races. When we accept that truth we can begin to think of community, of the oneness of the body of Christ. Otherwise we have a stratified church structure with each group developing without the influence and wisdom of the others. The youth and career and college men and women worship and serve in their areas, adults in men's and women's ministries, and the older adults in their specialized programs.

Some social scientists see the extreme divisions that we are presently promoting in school, church, and society as one of the ways we are driving youth into subcultures in search of intimacy and fulfillment of their dreams. In the worst situations, they have turned on their own kind in violent outbursts of destruction. The

In the Fig Garden Bible Church in Fresno, California, affiliated with the Mennonite Brethren Conference, almost one-third of the congregation are single adults—a blend of college students, single-parents, and professionals.

"I believe our significant number of singles is due in large part to the fact that we don't have a singles ministry," says the associate pastor, Marci Winans. "Our singles are fully integrated and involved in every area of leadership."

In this congregation the youth also serve the church body by taking turns in the nursery, children's church, and helping with vacation Bible school. Last year a senior college student directed the entire VBS program.
—Christian Leader, October 1999

numerous school shootings are one example of this.

In gentler situations, the youth lack a smooth transition into the adult Christian world after they are finished with supercharged youth activities. Some sit out for several years in somber silence, waiting to grow up, or for another high like marriage and family. Some never return. The awareness of a growing number of young adult singles in our congregations who lack a secure place, especially those without talents and gifts that can be used in public, should tell us that we are not doing something right. The church is a family only for some.

Look back before you look ahead. To reinterpret Peter's Pentecost sermon may mean a course correction in the church. But before we do that or even consider a new theological interpretation of a Scripture passage, we need to look back at our church life to ask ourselves whether God is blessing our present direction.

David Schroeder, seminary professor, reasons that unless

we are a people always looking back over our shoulder to see if God blesses, we will never be an interpreting church. In other words, every time we say as a body that God is redirecting our thinking we need to look back on what has taken place as well as forward to the new goal. There is no such thing as instant interpretation or authority to pronounce: "This is now what God wants of us."

It took several hundred years for the church to say yes to the radical view that people of color were whole human beings. Years of biblical interpretation, with extensive proof texts to underscore the old belief of the inferiority of some races, made change difficult. God has blessed the courage to make a course correction to accept all races as brothers and sisters.

The acceptance of women into the work of the church did not take place instantly but over many decades. Some congregations are still processing this change. Yet if we look back on this major change, it is invigorating to see how God has blessed women's gifts. Similarly, rethinking the role of the generations in the church needs a backward look as well as forward look. Have closely graded church structures added to or hindered the development of the kingdom of God?

Time shows the truth. Schroeder says that agreement on interpretation of Scripture can come only as we become a

In a class I taught in our congregation about turning points in life, we each did a spiritual life profile, charting on a grid the direction our inner growth had taken at various life stages. I found it significant that as we shared our stories a number of the class members mentioned that after high school, they drifted for a number of years until marriage and family. Then they again felt the need for Christian fellowship and returned to the church.

loosing (freeing from sin) and binding (binding oneself to what is above—Christ as Lord) community. We need to wait and see which of our interpretations God will bless—which ones are binding, which ones are freeing.

One group of those who heard Jesus teach and preach and do miracles denounced him as a false prophet. Another group acknowledged him as the Messiah. Time showed the truth. Time has also showed the truth with regard to women's ministries and the equality of all races before Christ. These have been freeing decisions. We can pronounce that God has blessed this change.

Do passages like Psalm 78, Joel 2, and Acts 2 offer a better way? Which emphasis will free young, old, and in between for greater ministry and service to the church?

Travel with me on a voyage of discovery to find out how the generations can find new respect for one another, cooperate, and together add strength of depth to the kingdom of God. Let me assure you, there is a lot going on. This book merely opens the door a little.

Now try this:

1. Establish a heritage committee with representation of children, parents, and grandparents. Interview both young and old and publish a book of the life stories of the oldest group.
2. Have someone prepare a slide show of congregational life, emphasizing the spiritual gifts of each age-group, to show to the whole body.
3. Examine some of the biblical stories of intergenerational relationships such as Abraham and his nephew Lot; Jacob and his sons and grandsons; Jethro, Moses, and his sons; the young Joshua's message to the elders; Ruth and Naomi's unique attachment; Eli, Hannah, and Samuel, a three-generation

spiritual relationship; Rehoboam and the elders; Timothy, his mother Eunice, and his grandmother Lois. Which factors in these relationships were freeing, which were binding?

4. Visit a cemetery with a group of children and imagine what life was like for the children buried there. How old were they when they died? What might they have died of? What facts can the children learn from the gravestones of adults buried there?

5. Help children memorize their lineage as far back as possible so that they will know they are a product of many ancestors. Some people joke about climbing the family tree, but that's all right. It is one way of bringing a sense of identity to children. One audacious woman drew her family tree on her eight-foot high living room wall, large, bold, and clear. It drew my immediate attention when I entered her home. What effect might such a diagram have on children to see a family tree rather than modern plastic wreaths and designs?

6. Hold an intergenerational art show with all ages exhibiting their work. A surprising number of older adults have discovered undeveloped artistic gifts after their retirement from work.

Chapter 2

Reconnecting the Generations

It is important for young and old to know, in a fundamental way, that every believer in Christ belongs to his body.

My mother had much time to reflect on her life as she grew older. She told me about her early life in Canada after emigrating from the Ukraine in the USSR in 1923. All the new arrivals were desperately poor and sometimes profoundly lonely for the old places and old ways. My parents lived in what I can only call a shack with two rooms. But because it was larger than the homes of most of the other immigrants in our tiny village, every Sunday afternoon they gathered there, adults and children. Needs of the spirit brought them together.

"We needed one another then," Mother told me. When the families grew into a more prosperous way of life, the gatherings became fewer. The gradual embracing of independence and material wealth pushed them away from each other. Mother mourned something she couldn't quite identify, but she knew it hurt.

I have pondered her story often. As these immigrants became emotionally and materially established in their new land, the ties that held them together became weaker. They lost the strong sense of community: the awareness that they needed one another.

Today, a growing movement in our society focuses on

the development of healthy intergenerational relationships between baby boomers and their elders, and between children, youth, and all those whose birthdays come before theirs. This movement says, "We need each other." It shows itself in such things as foster-grandparenting programs, and in architects' designs for intergenerational villages.

As we shall see in this book, the church has both the resources and some strong precedents to help it be a part of, and even lead, this revolution. We also need to celebrate the intergenerational learning that already goes on informally when school-aged children and youth visit their elders or interact with their grandparents. We must applaud every bonding of young and older spirits that makes becoming an adult a joy, and becoming an elder something to be looked forward to as a time of honor and privilege.

But we also need to recognize that there are big obstacles to overcome in bridging the generations. Our work, school systems, recreational activities, and media culture—all seem to keep the young and the elders in their own world. And the church is not immune.

Everyone in their slot

Next Sunday morning stand at the entrance to your church's sanctuary and watch what happens. Infants and toddlers are unloaded at the nursery, and each age-group of children is directed to a separate classroom. Youth, young adults, middle adults, and retirees all find their own places for the Christian education hour.

Examine the announcements for the coming church week. Youth meet Monday evenings, older adults on Thursday morning, and children on Wednesday evenings. Where do you see young, middle-aged, and old in a regular joint study, small group, or service project?

Watch what happens during the worship service. Children are either ushered out at the appropriate moment to their own worship service, or they go to the front for a story. The assumption is, "There will be nothing for them after the sermon starts. The material has to be on a child's level in vocabulary and content for them to get anything out of it." The result is that children rarely hear adults tell each other what faith means to them.

In the church, therefore, we may give the convenient appearance of community by being in the same building on Sunday mornings, albeit in different rooms. But too often, young and old aren't close, not because they don't like each other but because they simply don't know one another, especially in large churches. Each person functions individually in his or her niche in church life.

Dividing church ministries by age-groups, while sometimes practical and necessary, follows the pattern that defines our whole society, and which seems especially dominant in North America: generations kept separate. When I traveled in the former Soviet Union in 1989, I told my newfound relatives that I lived alone. They could not grasp the strange reasoning behind this living arrangement. Grandparents belong with their grandchildren.

Similarly, one of my professor friends, Dwight E. Roth, reports that his international students ask him, "How can the age-groups be so separate from each other in the United States? Where are the family values that Americans say are so important? The elders are to be cared for; they are the wise people who are to be honored." The students are puzzled.

An urgent agenda

Roth, who teaches sociology at Hesston College in

Kansas, has studied how our society is age-segregated from the cradle to the grave in education, in church, in workplaces, in volunteer groups, and in recreational activities. In an unpublished paper Roth wrote, "The long-term implications of this trend need to be discussed and acted upon. Relatedly, the postmodern world in which we live is increasingly segregated by age when, in fact, the generations need each other. . . . In our rapidly changing world we need to . . . anticipate the future."

To deliberately work toward bringing the generations together may be our last chance to bring wholeness to society.

A society without generational interconnectedness cannot thrive. Mary Pipher, in *Another Country: Navigating the Emotional Terrain of Our Elders*, offers a stark scenario. She writes that ten fourteen-year-olds grouped together will form a "lord of the flies" culture—competitive and mean. But ten people ages two to eighty grouped together will fall into a natural age hierarchy

When I was a child our family attended a very small church about twenty miles from home. It was attended mostly by new immigrants from southern Ukraine. The services and Sunday school were conducted in German. Our family had already become anglicized. On Saturdays I agonized over the Bible lesson which we children would be expected to read out loud in German. I practiced the pronunciation with Mother.

In Sunday school the next day I counted the people who had to read before my turn came and inwardly practiced my verse. Sometimes the teacher jolted me to attention by choosing a different person to begin the reading. What should I do now? There was no time to practice another verse. I understood very little. I remember even now, the kindness of one teacher who allowed me to read my verse in English. (continued)

Today some of my dearest memories are of that little German church and the high moments I experienced when we sang hymns together Sunday after Sunday, especially the closing hymn. The moment was holy.

Often the oldest man in the church would speak the closing benediction. Though I didn't understand the words, I felt at peace as he committed the way of this diverse group of people, sometimes facing a difficult week, especially during the Great Depression, to the Lord. He drew me from my small child's world into his adult world. He helped me structure my inner life. I felt the praise, joy, sometimes sorrow, and defeat expressed in prayer and testimony.

I grieve for children who never experience adult joy or pain because they are not present.

that nurtures and teaches them all. Pipher believes that we need to reconnect the age-groups for our own mental and social health. To deliberately work toward bringing the generations together may be our lost chance to bring wholeness to society, she says.

Why did the generations get disconnected?

It will take tremendous effort on the part of young and old to connect. The life experience of someone over the age of seventy who grew up without running water and slept in the same bed as a sibling, maybe even two siblings, for possibly a decade, is far removed from that of today's child. Children now often have their own room, and possibly bathroom, and can program a VCR before they are school age. For us to recover intergenerational nurture today, we must contend with at least seven hurdles:

Lack of precedents. The biggest problem may be that we have no recent precedents to guide us in this new journey.

A large and growing older adult population and a decreasing teenage demographic is new to history. In the early decades of this century, life was short, with life expectancy in 1900 at about 47 years in the United States. Today, people over 65 number about 13 percent, with possibly 10 to 15 percent more in the congregation. Four-generation families are not uncommon today as life expectancy has reached the early 80s for women and the late 70s for men.

All generations have few patterns for how to relate to the many new elders in their midst. It's easiest for both generations to shove the other generation to the side. The script hasn't yet been written for a new relationship between them. Everyone needs to improvise as we move toward connectedness.

The extended family does not exist for all. Some deny that the generations have lost touch because they believe the extended family is still in place for most people. While this may be a blessing that some families enjoy, Richard H. Gentzler Jr. and Donald F. Clingan in God's Challenge to Church & Synagogue write that the extended family as the norm is an over-romanticized concept. It never existed.

Here in central Kansas many Mennonite families can trace their roots back to 1874 when large contingents of immigrants from Russia arrived in the area. Today many of them have vast extended families. But that is not true for all.

When immigrants landed on American shores, many left close relatives behind. My mother, for example, came to Canada from Russia in 1923 with my father and my two sisters, leaving behind her parents and ten of her twelve siblings and their families. I never knew much about her extended family until I was an adult and researched my roots. I never once enjoyed the love of a grandfather on either side.

When African-Americans came to this land as slaves, they were often cruelly torn from parents and brothers and sisters. Asians often left families behind to work here for several years before sending for their families. As James Michener shows in the historical novel *Hawaii*, large contingents of Chinese men worked in Hawaii's pineapple fields for years before seeing their families again.

In this century the Great Depression drove families both east and west in search of a livelihood. Today young families are often moved by their companies to new and often strange places. Families live far apart from one another. Grandparents live separately, and often at a distance, in nursing homes, retirement villages, and extended care facilities. Where extended families exist, they are separated and often fractured.

Divorce and remarriage. Divorce and remarriage have increased the number of elders in a family but also further fractured the extended family. Some children have as many as eight grandparents and step-grandparents as the result of divorce and remarriage. Yet this does not necessarily mean they encounter more older adults in their daily lives in any meaningful way.

Financial independence of the elders. Add to these factors the greater financial independence of the elders that makes it possible for them to live separately. Some retired people pack their motor home and head for elder communities in warmer climes. This often means leaving children and grandchildren behind for months at a time. Those in search of warmer climes also leave their home churches, and enjoy Christian fellowship almost exclusively with other elders like themselves.

Many older adults are determined to maintain their own independence as long as possible, not burdening children with their care. They want to live alone, but are not always happy with the loneliness and emptiness it may bring with it.

Commercialization of age-graded religious education materials. Age segregation is reflected in and strengthened by the commercialization of religious education material. Sunday school teachers have many options for materials for each age-group, from preschool to adults. Just as Bibles, devotional aids, and worship materials are being packaged separately for men and for women, they also come in age-appropriate versions for each group. Children are therefore spared the difficult stories of Samson and his lover Delilah (Judges 16), or the stoning of Achan and his family.

What children read depends on the subjectivity of the writer. Few children gain an impression of the biblical whole or of the character of God as both loving and judgmental until they are adults. In school students are required to tackle difficult literary materials like the Middle English of Shakespeare. If all age groups gravitate only toward people and materials that are easily grasped, with little to stretch them, souls become impoverished and faith weakens.

Technological revolution. The technological revolution is seen by some as the greatest wedge dividing generations. The elders cannot provide continuity in this area because they are often learners themselves. Elders grew up without telephones (to say nothing of cell phones and pagers, which every busy person, including students, today must carry), the ability to buy airplane tickets and groceries on the Internet, or to keep personal finances in order with software programs like Quicken. Many are openly fearful of trying to master that dismaying array of windows, clicks, and cheery "You have mail" messages.

At the same time, all the elders' experiential knowledge may seem outdated and even quaint to a generation that knows how to control the computer world with a few clicks of the mouse. Here, clearly, the young are on top because they learn to use a computer in grade school, but they are at the very bottom if they confuse this technological knowledge with true wisdom in the art of living gained through life experience. With such varying degrees of experience, it is easy for the generations to stay apart.

Psychological differences. Psychologist Mary Pipher says that the truly great divide between generations isn't technology or the events they lived through. It's psychology, or the way baby boomers and their parents have each been wired. Many elders grew up without TV, in a communal culture where actions counted more than words, manners mattered, and authority could be trusted. They learned to keep their feelings to themselves. "Slights, annoyances, or upset feelings didn't carry much weight."

Boomers, on the other hand, embrace psychotherapy, or "the talking cure," wholeheartedly. Some think their parents' reluctance to express their feelings, even their affection, is "repressive, cramped." Pipher concludes that one generation's way of coping isn't better than another's, just different.

Our concept of community has changed

There is much in our information age that drives the

generations apart. Ironically, however, the growing separation of the generations has happened at the same time that the church has been on a quest for community.

During the 1970s, many Christians in North America insisted that the church needed to get back on track with the New Testament concept of *koinonia*, or body life. Individualism and institutionalism had been emphasized too long, they said. The church needed to regain the experience of being the body of Christ. Christians asserted this again and again in the words of the popular song: "We are one in the Spirit, we are one in the Lord." They were bold enough to experiment with worship forms. A theology of spiritual gifts was taught vigorously. Honesty and vulnerability were in. Hypocritical piety was out. Communal living was at the top of the list of corrections to make, giving rise to communal groups such as Chicago's Reba Place.

But the direction of the pendulum changed again. As the church swung in the direction of institutionalism for the sake of greater efficiency and effectiveness, new studies in Christian education advocated closely graded classes. Psychologist James Fowler instructed us that humans developed spiritually in stages just as they developed psychologically. Accordingly, it became more important for curriculum to be "age-appropriate."

How age segregation was affecting the church was not given much attention, because this much-admired age-group, the teenagers, a new concept from the 1950s, was growing in our consciousness. Their vitality, their readiness to color outside the lines, and their zeal inspired many in the 1960s and 70s. The commercial world didn't blink twice, but instead took advantage of teenagers' new money power to seduce them.

The youth were heralded as the future of church and society. No sacrifice was too great to make for them.

A friend tells the story of an event that profoundly affected his thinking about the church when he was in his middle teens. His congregation practiced foot washing, and, since he was a baptized believer, he was obligated to take part. But as the basins were passed down the row to every other man, he suddenly realized he was last in the row. The first person in the next row was a very old man. He would be expected to wash that man's feet and that old man would wash his. He was scared and perplexed. Yet as he knelt before the old man, removed his socks, and washed the knobby feet, he experienced a holy moment. A new understanding of community dawned on him. Christ's body consisted of all ages.

Before long another stage in life prior to full adulthood emerged: the "young adult," who remained a young adult sometimes into age 30 or more, trying to find him or herself. The age wave had not yet really started. It wouldn't start for several decades.

In all this, a return to individualism kept threatening the glowing vision of *koinonia*, and it continues to do so today. "Be good to yourself" proclaim the advertisers, and your spiritual life will follow suit. Religious television allows believers to remain within the privacy of their home to worship, interrupting the broadcast to check the roast and use the bathroom. People want the freedom to develop their spirituality according to their own preferences. Accountability to a body of believers isn't a consideration.

Salvation increasingly has become a private matter between the self and God, and not the self, God, and other believers. It has little to do with the format of a new community in Christ. Some drift in and out of the church and from church to church, tasting a little spiritual food here and a little there, hoping something will appeal to them. The relationship between believers is no longer seen as a holy thing ordained by God.

Richard Gentzler, in his book *Aging: God's Challenge to Church and Synagogue*, writes: "Persons of all ages living, growing, working, and playing together is a hopeful concept. Children receiving love and learning faith and values from older adults, and older adults experiencing a sense of being needed and enjoying the continuity of life are important aspects for any society. However, uniting the generations is not an easy task."

The time has come for greater connectedness

The navigator of a ship at sea regularly asks, "Is this ship still on course?" If the ship has veered off course, he or she directs the pilot to make the necessary correction. The time has come for the church to make a course correction by reestablishing and nurturing intergenerational relationships.

The psalmist writes that one generation shall commend God's works to another, telling of his mighty acts (Ps. 145:4). In this book I want to show you the reasoning behind the intergenerational movement in society. I want all age-groups to come out commending God's works to one another, not just to themselves.

Each generation brings unique skills or qualities to any intergenerational experience. Although it's true that wisdom doesn't always show up with age, elders are the "wisdom people," carriers of knowledge and insights gained over time in the skills of living. The young, on the other hand, bring with them energy and enthusiasm and a willingness to risk; elders, with their greater reluctance to move off the path of tradition, can benefit from those qualities.

Drawing the generations together will be hard, for it means revising long-held attitudes and philosophies about the way the body of Christ functions best. It will be hard because it may mean dismantling some long-established fences. To cut across traditions of separation, albeit new ones, may be more difficult than finding our way through the maze of new worship styles. Change comes slowly over time, but the time to begin has come.

It is time to recapture the vision of Isaiah, who admonished the Hebrew nation to "enlarge the limits of your home, spread wide the curtains of your tent; let out its ropes to the full and drive the pegs home" (Isa. 54:2 NEB). While these words were directed to the Jews to embrace the Gentiles, they also offer a vision to today's families to take others into their family and make it "friendly space" for all ages, all races, all social classes.

Not a program

Already I hear you asking: "Is this book about rearranging church structures, or developing ministry programs along different lines? Are you advocating new Sunday school classes with all ages from first grade to the very elderly? That seems silly. Present structures along age-graded principles seem effective, at least to a certain degree, so why fix something that isn't broken? Why mess with what has been finessed over the last four or five decades?"

A rich young synagogue leader came to Jesus on bended knee, imploring him to tell him what he should do to inherit eternal life. He was keen on being told what to do, for he readily admitted he had kept the commandments from his childhood. Jesus responded that he needed a change of heart, not another "to-do" item to add to his agenda.

If a church leader were to come to Jesus asking the

same question: "Good teacher, what must our congregation do to inherit eternal life?" Jesus' answer might be
similar: "Let go of your attachment to doing and follow
me." This book is about changing our attachment from
what we do to what we are—the body of Christ, which
includes all ages, all races, both sexes—everyone who
comes to Christ by faith.

Now try this:
1. Discuss intergenerational relationships one Sunday
   per quarter in each class or during one quarter.
   Assess your congregation as to how well the generations are integrated.
2. Discuss the terms used to describe people in the last
   third or quarter of life such as seniors, elders, golden-agers, aged, and so forth. What difference does it
   make what we call this group?
3. Combine children's, youth, and adult choirs for a
   performance.
4. Ask adults to join youth in the next work project.
5. One quarter each year invite all ages to join in intergenerational elective classes. What makes this a
   monumental undertaking for some churches?
6. Discuss one area of church life where you could
   build in greater flexibility and age irrelevance so that
   each individual's gifts for ministry would replace
   usefulness as determined by age.

Chapter 3

Anabaptist History Strengthens the Concept of Intergenerational Relationships

"By rejecting infant baptism, the Anabaptists not only raised believers baptism to the status of the only binding and valid baptismal act, they made the children the future bearers of the Anabaptist world of faith and life."

In an unusual source, *The New Republic* (Jan. 17, 2000), I found a sensitive discussion of martyrdom today. The basis for the article was the book *She Said Yes: The Unlikely Martyrdom of Cassie Bernall* written by Cassie Bernall's mother, Misty, about her daughter's sudden death at the hand of a fellow high school student in the Columbine High School killings.

Jean Bethke Elshtain, in her lengthy discussion of the book, comes forward with some amazing conclusions about the role of young people in historical accounts of martyrdom. She describes the horrible death of Perpetua and Felicitas of the early church. Joan of Arc was only 19 when she was burned at the stake. Eulalia, "the most celebrated virgin martyr of Spain," was 12. Her list goes on.

Elshtain mentions Martin Luther King Jr.'s use of schoolchildren in the civil rights marches despite vigorous dissent by the Southern Christian Leadership Conference about his strategy. The children were arrested by the thousands, and hosed and attacked by dogs. But King knew the power of the witness of their deed, and because he believed his cause was sacred, he went ahead and included children. They suffered as a result.

One of Elshtain's conclusions is that "spiritual age is not chronological age, and that great deeds can be done prior to the 'age of consent.'" The great deeds she includes in her historical survey suggest "the power of early formation and the strength of formative moral influences in the hearts, the minds, and even the bodies of the young." Cassie Bernall, she writes, seemed to be moving toward a recognition of the need for "a tough-minded spiritual life."

Adult believers. Anabaptist faith was originally an adult believers concept. Baptism referred to adult baptism. Baptism, the first Anabaptists in Europe insisted, was the sign of a fully self-conscious, mature decision to join the body of Christ. The emphasis was on adult believers because only fully knowledgeable and grounded persons were able to make mature faith decisions that might possibly lead to interrogation and death at the hands of the state authorities. The Anabaptists did not see children and youth as generally able to make decisions, such as Cassie Bernall made.

Anabaptists saw themselves as a "covenanting brotherhood." They covenanted with one another to faithfulness, to service, and to suffering, for imprisonment and death might come at any time. They practiced an aggressive discipleship, knowing it might lead to persecution. As in the early New Testament church, being a member of the body of Christ wasn't optional. You couldn't be a follower of Christ without being part of a community in which you were known, loved, and held accountable for your actions.

Teenagers were unknown. But adulthood began much earlier in the 16th century than it does today. A teenager who dangled in limbo between childhood and adulthood, waiting for physical, psychological, and spiritual maturity, didn't exist then. In an ecclesiastical ordinance dated 1584 and recorded in *Martyrs Mirror*, all males age 14 and up, females age 12 and up, were to renounce all heresy and promise with an oath to observe the Catholic faith, defend the Catholic Church, and persecute heretics.

Men and women were brought to trial after the age of accountability if they were involved in Anabaptist proselytizing or attending meetings. Pregnant women often were given slightly better care than other prisoners until the birth of the infant. Then they were brought to trial and executed. The child was given over to the state so that it would not be infected by Anabaptist "poison."

Consequently, youths as young as 13 or 14 sometimes joined the ranks of the martyrs. Eulalia, age 12 or 13, after much torture was executed. Pancratus, a youth of 14, was decapitated. Forty youths were stripped naked and thrown into a cold pool. A miller's boy was beheaded at age 16. These examples, all from the *Martyrs Mirror*, tell us that instruction and nurture of the faith was not restricted to physically mature persons. It began much earlier, although it is difficult to determine exactly how it took place in a society in religious upheaval.

Marion Kobelt-Groch, in her article "Hear My Son the Instructions of Your Mother: Children and Anabaptism," offers reasons why so little is available about how the younger generations came into the faith. She agrees that Anabaptists were primarily adults; children remained in the background because they were not baptized believers and the government interrogators were not overly concerned about them. She explains that the Anabaptists lacked theoretical concepts of education, and furthermore, the organized education of children did not take place. Children were not gathered into schools for religious instruction. Yet somehow they found the faith of their parents or neighbors through informal teaching.

C. Arnold Snyder and Linda A. Huebert Hecht's book *Profiles of Anabaptist Women: Sixteenth Century Reforming Pioneers* is another resource with new research to help us understand the relationship between the generations during that time.

Believers of infant baptism in the state church had the assurance that all children were members of the church and therefore had eternal salvation. Anabaptist parents of unbaptized children had no such security. She writes: "By rejecting infant baptism, the Anabaptists not only raised believers baptism to the status

Jacob Dircks and his two sons who escaped imprisonment in Utrecht fell into the hands of interrogators at Antwerp. They were together condemned to be burnt at the stake on account of living for the truth, not for any crime they had committed. On their way to their death, Dircks' youngest son, Pieter Jacobs, met them and threw his arms around his father's neck. He was seized by the authorities and thrown under the feet of the crowd following the prisoners. When the father and his sons had each been placed at a stake, he asked, "How is it, my dear sons?" Each replied: "Very well, my dear father." The father and sons were strangled and then burned.
—Martyrs Mirror, 724-5

of the only binding and valid baptismal act, they made the children the future bearers of the Anabaptist world of faith and life." Faith had to be a matter of choice at emotional and psychological maturity, not a state conferred at birth through baptism. The Anabaptist parents knew that all faith nurture of their children was entirely up to them or their newfound faith would die out with the next generation.

Anabaptist intergenerational relationships

Anabaptists believed that children before the age of accountability were protected by the grace of God. Ulrich Zwingli, early Swiss reformer, and those who attached themselves to the Anabaptist movement believed that children in biblical perspective were included in the covenant people of God. Pilgram Marpeck argued that infants were without guilt, for they lacked knowledge of good and evil. Menno Simons as a priest baptized children, but then, on the basis of his study of the Bible, decided the church fathers were misguided with regard to infant baptism just as they were regarding the mass. Baptism on confession of faith alone was scriptural. The "infant bath" the believers had received as young children was no baptism at all.

Young children of Anabaptists were therefore included in the covenant people of God, whether baptized or not, but at some point they had to decide for themselves. But this does not mean parents neglected their religious upbringing, although there was much variation in the way children were dealt with. Some parents saw a higher loyalty to God than to their children, who were in a state of grace, and deserted them to go elsewhere to teach and proselytize. They trusted in the children's tender age to save them from damnation. Others refrained from becoming Anabaptists because children became wards of the state upon the parents' imprisonment. Still others spent much time and energy nurturing their children. Grandparents are not often mentioned in *Martyrs Mirror,* probably because there weren't many three- or four-generation families at a time when life expectancy was low.

Scripture was central to the Anabaptists. The Bible was their spiritual food. It is impossible to do even only a cursory reading in *Martyrs Mirror* without being astounded by the wealth of biblical knowledge these martyrs had. Adults as well as young believers knew the Scriptures thoroughly and would put to shame many of today's believers. Cornelius Krahn writes in *The Witness of the Martyrs Mirror for Our Day,* that most of the Anabaptist witnesses of the covenant were simple laborers, many of whom learned to read and write when they accepted the message presented to them. "This changed their life completely and gave them the motivation to learn to read, to study the Bible, and to share this experience with others."

On one occasion in 1557 after two Anabaptists were strangled and burned, the officials determined also to burn their books, for the one man was a bookseller. When the books were perceived to be on fire, the people set up an uproar, causing the executioners to flee. The books were thrown to the crowd, who reached for them eagerly.

Jacques Dosie, age 15, one of many young Anabaptist believers who were interrogated, answered ably from Scripture, giving lengthy answers, for he "was old in knowledge of Jesus Christ." When facing the interrogator, these young people and adults quoted verse after verse in their defense. It is obvious that aggressive instruction in Scripture was taking place between the

In the year 1550, in the bishopric of Bamberg, two young girls received Christ by faith, were baptized upon their faith, and tried to live in the newness of Christ's life in them. They were imprisoned, tortured severely, and encouraged by severe means to renounce their faith. They remained faithful and steadfast during the entire trial whereupon they were condemned to death. Their persecutors, to mock them, placed wreaths of straw on their heads. One of the girls said to the other, "Since the Lord Christ wore a crown of thorns for us, why should we not wear these crowns in honor of him? The faithful God shall for this place a beautiful golden crown and glorious wreath upon our heads." They died steadfast in the faith.

generations in some form. The importance of biblical knowledge to maintain a staunch testimony is a needed lesson to learn from the Anabaptists.

Anabaptists believed in the priesthood of all believers. "You also, like living stones, are being built into a spiritual house to be a holy priesthood, offering spiritual sacrifices acceptable to God through Jesus Christ" (1 Pet. 2:5). Everyone, young and old, had the privilege of coming before God's throne in prayer. Whenever a young person made a confession of faith in Christ as Savior he or she became part of the "spiritual house" of God, the body of Christ and the family of God. He or she was expected to accept adult responsibilities, which meant the supreme sacrifice on occasion.

Today we encourage our young people to believe, even to be baptized, but often they are not integrated into the body of Christ until well after marriage. There is a view that they are too immature for the "hard meat" of the Word and the rigors of church life and service even though in high school they are taught many difficult academic concepts and encouraged to take on significant responsibilities in school life and community service.

Some young adults do not feel comfortable in adult congregations, unless there is a strong youth program that keeps them separate from adults in some areas of church life. One high schooler said openly, "I can't worship in a place where there are pews." When teenagers move into acceptable adult roles and responsibilities, which usually includes marriage and a job, they may return to church, to participate in congregational decisions, and accept service roles. Until then youth have the option of studying the Bible, praying, socializing, and serving mostly in the context of their own age-group.

The Anabaptists encouraged young believers to give a strong vocal testimony to their faith when confronting authorities. The strong testimony of Cassie Bernall before being shot in the Columbine High School killings has inspired young and old. It is a reminder of what often took place in the 16th century when young believers were brought before the magistrates. According to newspaper reports, Cassie's young killer allegedly asked her, "Do you believe in God?" When she replied in the affirmative, he shot her. Some people now herald her as a martyr, although some people now question whether she or another girl was asked the question. In a matter of minutes life became very serious for the high schoolers of Columbine. There was no time to sort out what they believed. Regardless of what it was, in the book about her daughter, Misty Bernall makes it clear that Cassie was on a spiritual journey away from superfluous thinking and doing.

Life was also serious business in Anabaptist days. To

be a believer meant you didn't know when your life might end. The generations discussed spiritual matters as some do today. According to *Martyrs Mirror*, parents encouraged a sense of spiritual calling in their children.

In a letter to his wife, prisoner Hans Symons admonished her to be a pattern to their children of all humility, obedience, and instruction in righteousness. He wanted her to talk to their children about life in Christ, while he, their father, was being held in prison and might be executed any day.

He wrote: "And take for remembrance the Maccabean mother, how she strengthened her children, that they should not forsake the law of God. . . . For better is one child that fears God, than a thousand ungodly children; yea, it were better to die childless, than to leave ungodly children behind."

He puts a biblical foundation under his thoughts by adding Jesus' words to his disciples, "Whoever forsaketh not everything, father, mother, sister, brother, wife, children, property, lands, yea, also his own life, the same is not worthy of me." Symons' rendition of this passage makes Jesus' list more inclusive by adding "wife" and substituting "property and lands" for "houses."

The Anabaptists set spiritual values above personal possessions. Many Anabaptists lost all household possessions and personal wealth when the state authorities moved in. They wandered far and wide to escape their persecutors. Children would have been aware of the material sacrifices their parents made for their faith.

Some new converts had sponsors, or what we today might call mentors. An interrogator asks one young man, "Who were your sponsors?" indicating that adults other than parents were involved in the nurture of the younger generation. One young boy testifies that a teacher taught him and encouraged him to study the Scriptures, warning him about persecution. Jan Wouters acted as a mentor to his youngest three sisters, admonishing them to honor their mother and father. Then their parents could rejoice because "their children have found delight in keeping God's commandments." "Children that do not fear God are to believing parents an affliction from the Lord, which cannot be healed."

Adult Anabaptists left a number of written spiritual legacies in the form of letters, hymns, and devotional writings. Anna Jansz of Rotterdam (1539), about to be drowned, gave her infant son Isaiah to a local baker, who promised to raise her child. She wrote a lengthy last will and testament bequeathing him her spiritual strengths. She advises her son to seek the kingdom of Christ among the persecuted, the poor, the downtrodden, and the despised. "Flee the shadow of this world; become united with God; keep his commandments; observe all his words to them; write them upon the table of your heart; bind them upon your forehead."

Jorisen Simons (1557) left a testament to his son Simon when he was imprisoned in which he tells of his

The oldest son of Adriaen Wens, aged 15, could not stay away from the place of execution on the day on which his mother was executed. He took his three-year-old brother with him and stood at a distance on a bench to watch the proceedings. When she was brought out, he lost consciousness and fell to the ground. Afterwards when the crowd had left, he searched through the ashes for the screw that had been fastened to her tongue to keep her silent, his only reminder of her life.

early life and expounds scriptural texts. The writing contains a large number of Scripture references. He warns against sects and false teachers and admonishes his son to learn, and to live a clean moral life.

The Anabaptists exemplified their faith through martyrdom. In the home, children would have heard their parents talking about neighbors and friends who were executed for their faith and would have witnessed the pain, fear, and soul-searching. They would have been present when government officials burst into a congregation or home with a great show of power and physical violence to take prisoners. Some children witnessed executions. American literature tells vivid stories of young African-Americans who watched lynchings and were forever scarred by the event. Such life-and-death experiences cannot help but have influenced Anabaptist children for or against the religious views of their elders.

Four hundred and fifty years later. Now, more than 450 years later, we still hold to believers baptism and the priesthood of all believers. But we have since nurtured, encouraged, and invited into our midst a group of "junior priests" and we're not sure what to do with them until they grow up. Scripturally, they're the real thing, for they believe in Christ. Anabaptists expected mature responses and behavior of young adults. We don't, probably because our culture allows the young an extended period of childhood and dependency on parents, sometimes well into their twenties. Elshtain in her discussion of Cassie Bernall speaks of this as "our culturally sanctioned perpetuation of an increasingly prolonged adolescence or pre-adulthood."

Even though adolescence is a fairly new concept in our culture, we encourage and allow the young to spend most of their time with people their own age in high school, in recreational activities, even in church youth groups. We keep pushing them together, enabling them to reaffirm immature worldviews without extensive adult input, especially that of the oldest generation. Peer input is often the strongest influence on a person's life. Elshtain points to the "tethering" of today's young people to "authoritative cultural forms" or to a "teen culture." Cassie Bernall was able to "de-tether" herself from this and choose a "tough-minded spiritual life" through a long accumulation of affirmations to other values.

Here and there, there are those who see a new kind of adherence, a Cassie Bernall kind of Christian emerging in the church, a kind not known in church in past decades. Joyce Parker says in a personal letter, "These young people are saying yes to Christ to follow him into difficult fearful situations. I am awed with what God is doing."

Like the role of the elderly, the role of young people in the congregation is not clear. Congregations endorse them heartily when they put on a lively program on a Youth Sunday, raise money for mission trips, and engage in some good works. But a well-articulated role for the young in the body of Christ is a fuzzy concept. They are not offered "fishes and loaves," or the bread of life, to use Elshtain's phrase, only conflict resolution experts and psychobabble of the secular culture.

Should youth take part in congregational meetings? If not, why not? Let's have good reasons for their absence. Should they be members of church boards and committees? Or should they remain an auxiliary body, often strong in faith, weak in theology, maybe even ethics, with a limited, if any, connection to the suffering aspect of the covenant of the Christian community? Should they be expected to contribute to the church budget and spend less on CDs and athletic shoes? Maybe even tithe to help pay for utilities and other operational expenses of the congregation as well as missions?

That the young believer has the responsibility to bear burdens, meaning not just those of friends but those of older generations, is unclear to them and their elders. Youth ministries sometimes becomes a parallel organization with parallel worship services under the leadership of a youth minister.

The same could be said of older adults. In some large congregations they, like the youth, have become almost a parachurch organization, with their own worship, their own fellowship activities, their own program of volunteerism, care, and nurture. Their role is also not clear.

Older generations are fearful of the young people's brashness, daring, exuberant spirit, outlandish clothing, and loud music, and troubled by their sometimes weak verbalizations of faith. They rejoice at their testimonies if forthright and clear, hoping that when they experience the stabilizing influence of marriage and family, they'll become full-fledged members of the church and pick up the burden of church and community life.

How can the old and young help each other to be the church?

George Konrad writes in *Living as God's Family*: "Nurture is not the parallel activity of a multitude of agencies; it is the church at work helping each and all to grow." The total life of the congregation, including relationships and general climate, has nurturing qualities. Stratification of church ministries into children's, youth, adult, women, and older adult or other configurations may simplify structures, but it can result in these ministries freewheeling at the perimeter of the church with only the Sunday morning worship to bring them together.

A time for self-examination. A congregation can begin to examine how close it is to being an intergenerational church by measuring itself against the markers listed above which characterized the Anabaptists. How well do young and old know Scripture? Could we answer people who ask us to give a reason for our faith?

Konrad suggests a number of ways to bring young and old together. He recommends an expansion of the idea of mentoring (to be discussed in chapter 12). He calls for an assessment of the forms and structures that guide the life of the congregation. How are ministries divided? Only by age? Or by other ways?

What is the structure of public events, particularly Sunday worship services? Who takes part, week after week? When the "women in leadership" issue was at its height, one church leader always made sure at least one woman took part in some way in worship, but not always the same way, to accustom the congregation to seeing women in ministry. Would that be a way to bring the young and the elders into the center of the life of the church?

How does the church make decisions together? A prior question is who comes together to make congregational decisions? Are youth invited? Are they free to share their thinking?

How does the church deal with sin and the sinner (binding and loosing)? How does the body of Christ assist one another in living a life of discipleship? Congregational discipline is rare today in many churches. Many older Christians have clear memories of congregational discipline that was harsh, unloving, and judgmental. So many of today's young Christians are unaware that accountability of behavior is part of being a member of the body of Christ.

How does the church fellowship? Who gathers

Another kind of intergenerationalism: In the Anabaptist world, the vision of the early Anabaptists may be weakened unless the older generation keeps telling their stories of love in exchange for evil. Cesar Moya, executive secretary of the Mennonite Church in Colombia, clarifies this well. He states that at the fifth Latin American Anabaptist Consultation held in Paraguay in February 1999, present were "grandparents" of Anabaptism in Latin America as well as "babes" who had just begun their walk with our 16th-century ancestors.

Moya adds, "The previous generation should feel satisfied to see a new generation of Anabaptists, who are committed to this vision of the church and its theology." But they should also feel challenged to provide tools and materials to help this new generation [which include

(continued)

together? Who sits with whom? Is that the best way? Who has socials? Government regulations now force new buildings to accommodate the handicapped, which usually also meet the needs of frail elderly. Do youth need special facilities so that they can put up their feet or lie on the floor?

John Driver in *Community and Commitment* writes that to review the New Testament suggests that today's traditional concepts of community or fellowship or communion are greatly impoverished. "*Koinonia* is more than meeting together from time to time; it is more than merely enjoying the presence of others; it is more than those feelings of well-being which warm our hearts when we greet our friends at church functions; it is more than common ethnic, cultural, linguistic, and historical ties; *it is more than the organization of a congregation into a series of subgroups related to interest, age, and sex*" (my emphasis). Such multiplication of activities can become a substitute for true koinonia. He defines koinonia as consciously, by design, sharing what we have in common—the life of Jesus Christ.

As our congregations focus on building an international community without respect to race or gender, may we turn our attention to also building an intergenerational community in a culture in which the generations are becoming more distinct and separate. Ephesians 4 states that the walls of partition have come down in Christ Jesus. It's time to think of another kind of wall to come down—those that separate because of age. Change is effected when people hang in for the long haul. "Websites and rallies will not do it alone. Conversion experiences, without the sturdy wisdom of traditions and institutions, will not suffice," writes Elshtain. It will take one individual after another moving closer together.

Our information about intergenerational relationships in Anabaptist times is admittedly limited, yet the Anabaptists' readiness to allow the spiritually mature young into the community of suffering is significant.

young and old] develop an Anabaptist vision at the dawn of the 21st century. He asks who will replace key Anabaptists in the South American church when they step down.
—Mennonite World Conference Newsletter Courier, Second Quarter, 1999

Now try this:
1. Should we expect more of young people? How can they be encouraged to become more fully integrated in all aspects of church life? Should we expect more of elders?
2. Have an intergenerational group share in small groups their experience of baptism or foot washing. What aspects were meaningful?

In 1552 a youth called Cornelis van Julenburg was imprisoned for three years for his testimony of Jesus. During his imprisonment he was verbally and physically tortured by priests, monks, and prelates. They laid snares for him, offering him worldly enticements to recant. But he resisted and was tied to a stake. While there, the priests again tried to make him give up his faith but he chose to die rather than to depart from the truth, "thus becoming a partaker of the sufferings of Christ" (Martyrs Mirror, 538). *He sounds like an early Cassie Bernall.*

3. If you knew you were about to die, what spiritual legacy would you want to pass on to your children and grandchildren? Consider writing a spiritual will to be placed in your safe deposit box together with your will disposing of your material possessions.

4. Try a mock trial in the manner of the interrogators in Anabaptist times. Use some of the same questions they asked. How well would you be able to defend your position?

Chapter 4

Stereotyping: The Enemy of Relationships

To dump all people of a certain age into one category robs them of their individuality and dignity.

A rabbi asked his students, "How can we determine the hour of dawn, when the night ends and the day begins?"

One student suggested, "When from a distance you can distinguish between a dog and a sheep?" The rabbi answered "No."

"Is it when one can distinguish between a fig tree and a grape vine?" asked a second student. The answer again was no.

"Please tell us the answer then," said the students.

"The hour of dawn is when you look into the face of human beings and you have enough light to recognize them as your brothers and sisters. Up until then it is night, and darkness is still with us," said the wise teacher.

A friend commented that he had watched students at the church-related college where he taught rush through the cafeteria line on the day when community elders came to the college to attend an enrichment series. One student commented he didn't want to get caught behind "a slow older person," let alone look her in the face.

A 70-year-old commented he didn't get too close to

teenagers for fear he'd chase them away. He was sure their reaction would be "What does this old man want from me?" But he hadn't tested his thinking.

A group of high schoolers acted out a skit in church that featured a number of old people. I was amused how they portrayed them—cane (of course), shuffling steps, trembling movements, and hats, shawls and long beads on the women. They dangled handbags with short handles. I thought of friends my age and older who jog and wear fashionable clothes (including all styles of handbags).

My reading and experience shows that younger generations often stereotype older adults as inflexible, passionless, and grumpy old bores. They're sickly, sexless, ugly, and disengaged from life. They don't know how to dress attractively. Their speech got frozen in the jargon of their own teenage years. They all wear false teeth and hearing aids and are constipated old stick-in-the-muds worried only about getting bran flakes for breakfast. The current TV commercials of two older women arguing about trivialities related to storing gravy in plastic bags depicts this stereotype well. If a boomer generation were speaking, some might add comments about their elders as being unproductive and burdensome, needing strong financial and emotional support. And aspects of this may be true.

Some younger generations simply shove all people over retirement age into one broad category. I was asked to fill out a questionnaire about church participation. At the top I was asked to circle my age, listed by decades. But the last age listed was 60. I added 70, 80, and 90. I hesitated to include 100 since I didn't know anyone that age. The slipup was unintentional but revealed how easily we drop people into categories. Whoever made out the questionnaire automatically put everyone over the age of 60 into one broad group, not realizing that at present even in retirement centers the residents are easily grouped by age—young old, middle old, and frail elderly.

In society at large, the loud message is to get rid of the signs of aging. Run to the stylist at the first sign of gray, work at body sculpting, and indulge in anti-wrinkle cream. The message is clear that to show signs of growing older demonstrates defeat.

Robert Butler, author of *Why Survive?* coined the term for stereotyping of elders as "ageism." It is the process of systematic stereotyping of and discrimination against people because they are old. He protested that age or the physical signs of aging are a poor predictor of health and vitality, of work status, of family situation, and the strength of creative urges or the degree of productivity. In reality, aging can't be measured by years. It varies from person to person.

Young parents have expectations of their children's development—what they can expect when the infant will hold up its head, roll over, babble, say a few words, and so forth. But even those standards don't always spell normal development. Some children develop more slowly, some more quickly, and yet all are in the normal range. Similarly, it is impossible to predict decline for elders in terms of toothless at 70, arthritis at 75, deaf and forgetful at 80. "He's still thinking clearly at age 90," people utter in amazement as if people this age who have alert minds have moved off the achievement chart to become gray-haired wonders.

Ageism has deep roots

The earliest image of aging comes to us from the Old Testament and from folklore. The elders in a society were the sages, prophets, leaders, and conveyers of wisdom, sources of knowledge, and the keepers of memory and tradition. They were revered in society.

The early Israelites were instructed to "Rise in the presence of the aged, show respect for the elderly and revere your God. I am the Lord" (Lev. 19:32). When Jeroboam and his followers came to Rehoboam and asked for easement of the burden placed on them by the king, King Rehoboam rejected the advice of the elders who had served his father Solomon. They advocated leniency. Rehoboam turned to the young men who had grown up with him and were serving him. They advised him to make the burden heavier. He was to tell them: "My father scourged you with whips; I will scourge you with scorpions"(2 Chron. 10:1-15).

As the prophet Elisha went up to Bethel, a large gang of youths came out of the town and jeered at him. "Go on up, you baldhead!" Elisha turned around and cursed them in the name of the Lord. Two bears came out of the woods and mauled forty-two of them (2 Kings 2:23-25).

Passages such as these were key stories in forming a theology of aging in the minds of many of today's elders. They heard these stories again and again in Sunday school. They knew it was a bad thing to poke fun at older people. It was almost innate to stand and give your chair to an older person.

As some of that reverence for the elderly was lost over the years, a new public image of old people emerged as poor, sickly, senile (Alzheimer's had not yet been identified), and especially grumpy and unattractive. Most of these people knew the euphemism "golden agers" didn't apply to them. Maggie Kuhn, activist for all older people, satirized the elderly as being kept in glorified playpens. Old people were "put" into old folks homes, as in "We put mother into a home," as if she were an object that needed storage for a time.

Before the early 1980s, real older people were underrepresented or missing in movies or television. If present they were cute, comical, pathetic, and/or incidental to the plot. Women were unattractive, frumpish, and often befuddled. Older men outnumbered older women three to one. Proportionately more older characters were bad characters, especially older men. More older women were portrayed as victims and in poor health.

As Social Security began to kick in and as the number of older people increased, the image changed again about the 1980s to reveal older adults as wealthy, hedonistic, selfish persons. Politically they were unstoppable. Grandparents became lovable. Older women were portrayed as powerful, creative, appealing, and affluent. Think back to television shows like *Dallas, Murder She Wrote, The Waltons,* and the *Golden Girls.*

During this period older adults also became known as discount grabbers, greedy geezers. The new euphemism was "senior" or "senior citi-

A friend who enjoys going to Branson, Missouri, an entertainment center much patronized by older adults, told me that at only one theater, of the many in the area offering topnotch entertainment for mature consumption, it is not unusual to see 60 to 70 buses lined up outside after depositing their riders. The sight of that many buses was clear evidence of the discretionary income available to this age-group. It also showed their search for new experiences to fill their time and for meaningful ways to spend their money. Is it also because they have no clear call from church and society that they are needed once they have retired?

zen," although all the seniors knew that the term applied to them didn't mean anything more than a discount at McDonalds, not the power associated with being a senior pastor or senior vice president.

Some of today's movies and commercials have improved in their portrayal of elders, but others still uphold the stereotype of the older man as distinguished, good-looking, and attracted to young women. Elizabeth Markson, director of the gerontology center at Boston University, screened 350 movies to study how elders are portrayed. She concluded: "Older men can be anything from stockbrokers to spies to pool sharks to cowboys."

And older women? They tend to be fairly negatively portrayed. Often they're shown as being lonely, or not having much of a family life, states Jake Harwood, another communication researcher from the University of Kansas.

A 23-year-old actress, commenting in the *Wichita Eagle* this past year said, "The idea that being an older woman is this terrifying and gruesome thing that happens to you, and you become completely undesirable—it's something you really internalize!"

Often if older women are portrayed, they are completely touched up to the point of not showing even a single wrinkle. Norma Zimmer, the champagne lady of Lawrence Welk's popular musical show, hasn't been allowed to age in several decades except for a slightly tremulous voice. Her face still looks as smooth as it did forty years ago. Advertisers project the image that looking one's age is bad because so much of their ad revenue comes from people who would go out of business if the visible signs of aging were esteemed in our society, says Linda Van Grinsven in *Priscilla Papers*.

A newer and more positive image is developing of our elders as alert, agile, with all faculties intact, willing to serve and to learn, able to care, and affirming life. This is the image that needs endorsement.

Stereotypes keep the generations apart. The young are seen as nipping at the heels of the older people and a threat to their control and authority. Handing over the controls is viewed as a threat to one's authority. Mentoring is the answer to this fear. Trust in God's presence in life and the strong awareness that God has a role for the older adult allows for the handing over of power with peace of mind. Evelyn Eaton Whitehead and James D. Whitehead write in their book *Christian Life Patterns*, "A greater trust in God's presence in life allows me to see younger colleagues not as threats to my authority and harbingers of my obsolescence but as companions with whom I share control and responsibility."

Mature Christians can trust that the Holy Spirit is with the church from generation to generation. This trust accepts that the next generation will alter what is handed to them—the institutions the elders carefully and at great sacrifice built up and their particular view of the faith.

A good example comes from the life of Mennonite leader Harold S. Bender. He is recognized for having presented the Anabaptist community with a renewed perspective of the Anabaptist Vision. *Mennonite Encyclopedia* describes him as the "leading Mennonite spirit in his time, ca. 1932-62." Among the key elements of Bender's vision were discipleship, a renewed church with voluntary membership, separation from the world, and love and nonresistance applied to all human relationships.

Now some 40 years later, Gerald Gerbrandt, president of Canadian Mennonite Bible College, challenges the Anabaptist community today to "reimagine the Anabaptist vision." Without denigrating Bender's vision, he dares to say Bender's vision is no longer adequate. In his essay in *What Mennonites Are Thinking 1999*,

Gerbrandt writes that Bender's vision was shaped by the context, needs, and dangers of the time for which it was written. If Bender were alive and able to watch this tinkering with his statement, how would he feel? I hope he would encourage such new work on the theology he developed, yet not all older generations can handle with grace change to the theologies, institutions, and programs they developed at great sacrifice.

How does stereotyping of the elderly show up?

Language. Stereotyping is apparent in our language: "There's no fool like an old fool" has been pronounced over many an older man courting a younger woman. "You can't teach an old dog new tricks" has convinced too many elders that it is too late to learn a new skill. One older man gave up his job for early retirement rather than learn to use the computer.

Terms to denote elders have changed. Why the resistance today to being called "old"? Because the connotations of the word "old" are unpleasant: outmoded, useless, deficient, antiquated, on the shelf, over the hill, old coot, old crock, and little old lady in tennis shoes. The apparent opposite of old is young, fresh, modern, fashionable, forgetting that young also means untried and inexperienced.

Housing and employment. It shows up in housing discrimination practices (adults only, a rule often reinforced by the adults themselves) and in employment practices (refusal to hire retirees except in low-paying jobs like department store greeters and carryout employees).

Attitude toward sexuality. When the sexuality of older adults comes into the conversation, it is often with a snicker and the snide assumption: They can't still be doing it. Though we may affirm the sexuality of all people, we tend to desexualize older adults. Yet they have sexual feelings, sexual needs, especially needs for affection. From the book *Sexuality and the Sacred*: "Faithfulness to the gracious God who has created us for wholeness requires that we affirm . . . the possibility of securing sexual justice for older adults . . . of reclaiming God's gift of eros for persons of all ages."

Christian commitment. In the Christian community we stereotype both young and old by an unspoken belief that passionate decisions for Christ are made early in adult life and few, if any, when you are in the last quarter or third of life. H. Newton Maloney in "The Graying of America" offers the opinion that the church at the turn of the century will need to prepare for many first-time decisions among its older members.

Conversions in the afternoon of life did not happen early in life in the previous century because people did not live long enough to become reflective. Now, with the added gift of years, they have time to change. Many elders will become unselfish for the first time in their lives. Maloney concludes that "it will be tragic if the church of tomorrow assumes the elders want only to be served and not to be of service." The same could be said of attitudes toward youth.

A negative public image. The more a society yields to negative stereotyping, the more negative the public image of the age-group becomes. A public image is the shared interpretation of the realities of a particular group. C. S. Lewis accused modern persons of "chronological snobbery"—the conviction that whatever is newer must be better than what is older.

Youth are stereotyped too

Butler's term "ageism" isn't usually applied to teenagers but I propose it should be. We degrade both the elders and the young by seeing them as people who are treading water, waiting for something, unproductive, and burdensome.

If young people fail to see the differences in their elders, older people likewise drop teenagers they don't know personally into one big pot. Teenagers wear crazy hairdos, the boys keep their caps on—even in church services. They wear outlandish clothes with pant legs dragging the floor and bodies pierced in the oddest places like a pagan. They're always chattering on the telephone or listening to outrageous music. They speak a language impossible to understand.

They're irresponsible and can't be depended on to carry through with a task. They're messy, foul-mouthed, and disrespectful to adults. They're always digging in the refrigerator. They don't like old people. They shriek at rock concerts like a passel of blue jays at a city dump. The tendency is to forget that youth are a product of their times, just as older adults are a product of their times, and that not everyone is the same.

High school is day care for teenagers. Richard A. Melcher in a radical view suggests that our society stereotypes teenagers by not expecting enough of them. Because of the time spent together and their focus on the media, they have more in common with each other than with adults in their lives. He suggests we should abolish high school and start secondary education in seventh grade and end it after tenth. Then release the kids at age 15 or 16 so they can get a faster start on the rest of their lives. Too extreme?

Melcher's main concern is that society treats

teenagers like children, so that segregated from the rest of society, they "turn obsessively toward each other, forming cliques and agonizing over who is most popular or beautiful or cool." He states that high school wasn't always considered a near-mandatory rite of passage. As recently as 1940, less than 50 percent of the adult population had gone beyond the eighth grade. Now, nearly 90 percent of adults age 18 to 24 have a high school degree. He describes high schools as holding pens—a series of pep rallies, pop quizzes, proms, and field trips. Introduce them to the real world sooner, he advocates. "The new century beckons."

Leo Botstein, president of Bard College in Anandale-on-Hudson, New York, is the best-known advocate for abolishing high school. In an article in *Business Week,* he argues that the high school overhaul should be accompanied by higher expectations, forcing graduates to be adept in everything from civics to economics. For those who don't want to attend college, apprenticeships, public service, or vocational schools should be options.

Stereotyping is with us all the time.

To dump all people of a certain age into one category robs them of their individuality. There is no one typical teenager as there is no one typical elder. Each is an individual in God's sight, responsible for his or her own sin, salvation, and service. Stereotyping prejudges and robs people of respect. Stereotyping denies individuals the respect they deserve regardless of age and replaces the ability of an individual to function effectively by his or her number of birthdays.

Stereotyping is sometimes subtle, sometimes blatant. When youth are placed on a cultural pedestal, they influence the economy powerfully. As older adults take over a larger percentage of the population, the consumer economy will skew in their direction. It always moves swiftly toward the population with the most potential for purchasing consumer goods.

When we define individuals by chronological age rather than by their character and individual features, we refuse to give this group a moral, cultural, and spiritual role in church and society. The hurdle we face today is that roles for both elders and youth are unclear.

To define someone between the ages of 13 and 19 as a "teenager" instead of as a student or other term highlights their age and all the connotations that emotionally charged word brings with it to the mind of the listener. Teenagers are expected to be irresponsible, to have messy bedrooms, and to shatter windows with high-decibel music.

To define someone over the age of 65 as a retiree or even senior denies that person other identities. To use the term "retired teacher" clearly states that person is finished with teaching. The term says also that this person is not now what he or she used to be (i.e., A retired teacher is not a teacher).

Even while I maintain that stereotyping is inappropriate, the evidence of our eyes and ears tells us that the older population does have some characteristics in common: they are more likely to be sick, more likely to be near the end of life, more likely to be dependent, and to think in terms of limited time. Everyone will eventually have membership in this group.

Youth likewise have some characteristics in common: They are more likely to have energy and a readiness to risk, more likely to think in terms of life opening up to them, more anxious to try independence, and to think in terms of limitless time for exploring their life options. Many are deeply concerned about others' needs.

The solution is to admit that all young people share some features despite their diversity, just as all elders share some characteristics. If in church and society we stress only what each age-group has in common we fall into the evil of stereotyping. Therefore it is important to recognize both traits of young and old as groups, yet recognize individuality.

How can we bridge the divide?

Acknowledge that everyone is made in the image of God. The end of stereotyping is to see everyone, young or old, or in between, as made in the image of God. The unhappy, crabby old woman and the "I-dare-you-to-tell-me-what-to-do" young person were both made in God's image. God invested in Jesus Christ for both of them.

Learn to know one another. We can end stereotyping by learning to know one another better in as many settings as possible. This was true when women first became pastors. A neighbor confided in me that when her congregation hired a woman as pastor, her hackles stood straight up. She was determined not to like her. Yet as she got to know her as a sister in Christ, especially in her pastoral role, her attitude changed. She now supported this woman wholly.

One pastor in Wichita goes to lunch at the school across the street every Monday to talk to students from his church. He tries to get out to support his students as much as he can, whether it's at lunch, sporting events, concerts, or plays. "It's hard to make a difference in kids' lives when you just see them once a week," he states. Prayer alone is not the answer. There has to be interaction and it has to be intensive.

Another man mentions the barrier between himself

My moment of truth came when my grand-mother had a stroke, yet remained in her home for a time. She was partially paralyzed and could not talk. She was also incontinent. Once when I visited her with my parents, I was volunteered to help Mother and my aunt change her. I recall the rush of feelings as I helped: revulsion, for an aging sick body is a human being at its earthiest; sorrow that Grandma would never again laugh so hard her belly shook with emotion; and awe as I sensed that I was standing in the presence of the end stage of life's cycle and return to one's Maker. Soon after that she was taken to a nursing home where she died.

and the elderly in a nursing home where his dying mother lived. He first saw these people as a static class, born that way. "After a time as friendships deepened, I saw them as me. I saw myself in them, and I saw myself in their faces and in their life struggles."

Learn about aging. In addition to information about careers, starting and establishing a family, and handling family and marital conflict, youth need to observe at close range what life will be like when they are 65 or 90. They need to learn how to cope with crises like death and sickness as well as smaller losses, like lessening eyesight or hearing.

As youngsters we got our information about the birds and the bees and what happened in the cabbage patch mostly from cloakroom talk, surreptitious reading, and eavesdropping on the conversation of our elders. We pieced together enough facts to begin adulthood. Unfortunately, information about their elders gets picked up by the young in much the same way unless they have close contact. It comes to them from advertising, movies, reading, and maybe from a disturbing single visit to an elderly relative in a nursing home.

Persons in each stage of life get their attitudes toward the aging process from those who are modeling it. Youth and middle adults may watch what is happening to only a small segment of the elderly and think all older people are sick, unhappy, and lonely. They are unaware that most of the elderly are well, enjoying life, and contributing to it. Older adults need help to fit together the many little bits of wisdom and knowledge they have gleaned from life. They need to be assured that the discomforts, perplexities, and losses they experience as the afternoon of life moves into the evening are as normal as the anxieties of the adolescent in his or her first infatuous relationship.

Think before we speak. I propose we withdraw from linguistic currency two popular words. One is "retiree," a killer word someone has said, because it encourages withdrawal from life. The other is "teenager" because it connotes frivolity, self-centeredness, and a passion for consumer goods. When we change our language we also change our attitudes toward the referent. What words to use in their place? Transitioner for the one group? Youth for the other?

Words have a negative, positive, or neutral connotation, a very important aspect to poets and other types of creative writers. One word with the wrong connotation can throw a whole poem off. Our language reflects and affects our attitudes toward the object we are speaking about. The person who controls language is the person with power. At one point President Bill Clinton threatened to define nicotine as an addictive drug. Such a ruling would shift power to government, away from ciga-

This week look for positive and negative images of both adolescents and older adults in advertisements, movies, television shows, and newspaper reports. For example, in a story about a losing basketball team, how are the athletes referred to by the coach and reporters if they are in high school? In college? Why speak of college players as "kids" and "youngsters" when they lose a game, but as adults when the same aged person pulls a gun and injures someone?

In a story about older adults, why is the woman referred to as grandmotherly but the man never as grandfatherly? Why are older women sometimes jokingly addressed as "young lady" as if a compliment is being offered?

Women in our society are considered old at a younger age than men. It is not unusual to see a wife with dark hair sitting beside her husband of the same age whose hair has turned quite white. Study advertisements that
(continued)

rette manufacturers. Several decades ago, black men objected to being referred to as "boys" by white men. Female employees said no to being called "girls" when they were 50 or more years of age. The language of nomenclature tore down their self-esteem. What we call elders and youth is important.

Examine the media. Who can forget the somewhat appealing advertisement featuring an elderly Clara Pella. She stalks into the fast-food restaurant demanding loudly, "Where's the beef?" while holding up the two halves of her empty bun. Or the older man, obviously courting the older woman, sheepishly stirring up cappuccino without a machine to impress her. In these and other similar advertisements, elders are depicted as idiosyncratic and not the kind of people you would like to have around.

If elders think that society, especially younger generations, see them as useless, unproductive, dull creatures, they think of themselves the same way. People with power determine our identity or self-concept.

Distancing oneself from elders through stereotyping allows for avoidance of an aspect of life that is feared. Children want to grow up. Middle-aged people seldom say, "I want to grow old" because the public image of old age does not appeal.

Change is coming. Ken Dychtwald predicts in his newest book, *Age Power*, that economic and political clout will shift from the young to the old. He also says that boomers "are beginning to look down the road a little bit. They are beginning to notice people a little older. . . . And checking out how these older people are doing." He writes, "My guess is that they will transform old age into an attractive, cool stage of life."

emphasize appearance. What kind of appearance is extolled for older adults to remain "youthful"? For young people to look "cool"?

Read fairy tales that include older adults such as Cinderella, Snow White, and Hansel and Gretel. What are the dominant characteristics of adults in these stories that an older generation grew up with?

Now try this:

1. Intentionally construct a positive public image of both elders and adolescents in the congregation through public rituals and modes of communication which involve all age-groups and many kinds of symbols and traditions (see chapter 11).
2. One person who works in a retirement community said he would like to see the myth shattered that old age is the richest part of life—that these are the "golden years." He has worked with many elderly people and they all say that the last half is not neces-

For his master's thesis (1981) Dwight E. Roth, professor of sociology at Hesston College, Hesston, Kansas, compared two ethnic communities, the Yoder Old Order Amish Church and the Hesston Mennonite Church, both in Kansas. He interviewed both aged and nonaged (under 64) members in each congregation, one of which would be considered modern and progressive and the other conservative. Significant comparisons between the two congregations emerged.

He found that in the Amish church, the family played a central role in the community. Obligations to the family took precedence over individual desire and choice. Membership was counted in terms of families, not individuals. They believed in transgenerational leadership. The age range of church leaders in the district he studied ranged from 31 to 89. The Amish elders saw
(continued)

sarily the best half. In some respects it is as hard to be an elder as a youth. He believes that each segment of life has its own merits and follies. How do you respond?

3. Have youth list their stereotypes of elders, honestly, if possible. Have elders do the same for young people. What did you learn?

4. Have a few elders tell young people how they reinvented their lives at key points and changed their thinking about clothing styles, music, cars, and sexuality.

5. Ask your group to keep track of television portrayal of elders. Are they central to the show? intruders? meddlers? patronizing? dependent or independent? capable? How are high schoolers portrayed?

6. Have elders teach young people a skill, such as whittling, making an ethnic dish, bird-watching, or embroidering.

7. Have each child select one interesting elder in the

church and community and prepare a short biographical sketch after interviewing the person.

8. Analyze songs, hymns, and poems that have growing older as the theme: "When You and I Were Young, Maggie," "Silver Threads Among the Gold," "Grow Old Along with Me," "Sixteen Was a Very Good Year," "Crossing the Bar" (Tennyson), and "Fear Death" (Browning). What do they say about aging? We have special hymns for children. Should we have hymns for each age-group?

their adult children as having a duty toward them. They believed they were respected for their wisdom. The Amish elders said, "It's good to have a mix of age in church leadership. Youth has vitality and energy. On the other hand, age has caution because of life experience."

In the Mennonite Church the age range of leaders in the district was from 22 (youth pastor) to 58 (board member). The aged Mennonites generally saw themselves as potential burdens to their children. They were hesitant to make the same assertion as the Amish that they were respected for their wisdom. One woman noted that "we are put in the backseat of life and not respected." The Hesston elders stated they had no official influence because there were no elders in leadership in the congregation.

How would your congregation respond in a similar survey?

Chapter 5

Let No One Despise Your Age

The church has a gold mine of wisdom, courage, and stability in its pews that is worth much more than winning at bingo, computer games, Jeopardy, or similar activities that emphasize trivia.

When I was a young married woman, I lived in a community where occasionally the churches gathered to hold an *Altenfest* (festival for old people). By definition it was for people who considered themselves old. I wish I had attended at least one or two of these fests to find out what the preachers talked about.

Did the gatherings promote a security-type faith—peace, comfort, strength for the journey—or did they encourage pioneering faith: adventuresome, abundant, joyful? I doubt that the roles the elders played in church and society were discussed.

At that time the concept of roles was unfamiliar. As you aged, you subsided into a sideline spectator role waiting for life to finish its course.

A major task for the church in the new millennium will be to define stronger positive roles for the growing number of active elders and to deliberately seek ways to work out these roles in a world accustomed to having the old folks retreat to their own pursuits once they retire. In this new century, with the boomers edging toward the category of elders, to wait another 10 to 20 years will be too late to pay attention to this task.

I've long wanted to see our elders thought of as people you do things with, not for. I am convinced that though the older adult can't teach young people much about modern technology, their gift is the wealth of their experience of years, wealth that should expand with age.

They've experienced childhood, adolescence, young adulthood, middle-age, and retirement. They are 40 to 50 years ahead of the game when compared to young people, which should give them a psychological edge. Sometimes it doesn't. Just as some college students leave college untouched by four years of new information, some elders have lived the same year over for 50 years.

Psychologist James Hillman writes: "Things seem to gain in value as they get older, whether or not they're useful or beautiful, but we deny this same appreciation to old people. Our society has had a renewed interest in antiques in recent years. A piece of furniture, a picture, a vase, is valued for its oldness, for the cherished patina life has given these objects. A chest is particularly valuable if someone wrote on the lid the names of the original maker and to whom it was presented."

Hillman writes that the old face is not regarded as something "beautiful, important, or valuable." He asks how this absence of images that represent "depth, wisdom, suffering, or passion—the power and intensity of being old" affects society.

Beauty is equated with young people with smooth skin, supple limbs, and a full head of hair. By implication the old are ugly and not valuable. Their life experiences do not increase in value but are diminished.

When the church has no specific role that incorporates respect and dignity for its older adults, aging becomes a sign of obsolescence and despair. Aging carries no message of light to the younger generations. Older adults are not seen as the crown of the congregation, but as a group of people to be pitied and taken care of physically and economically. The wisdom, stability, values, and courage of the elderly are left untapped. Consequently, both old and young suffer.

The church has a gold mine of wisdom, courage, and stability in its pews that is worth much more than learning how to win at electronic games, *Jeopardy*, or similar programs that emphasize trivia. Hillman sees aging as a positive state. In his book *The Force of Character and the Lasting Life*, he states that aging, in itself, may be doing something for us, not merely something to us. While some people promote physical longevity without adding the spiritual dimensions, he promotes the view that aging is necessary to the human condition. It is essential for the growth of the soul. I agree. God had something in mind when people age.

The role of wisdom bringers

The elders in our society used to be the keepers of memory and the storehouses of knowledge and wisdom, giving life continuity. They provided basic knowledge of how things were to be done from baking bread to holding a funeral service. They were the encouragers. These functions have now been replaced by other types of sources—especially radio, television, magazines, and newspapers. Advice is dispensed by columnists from the medical field to child rearing. Each evening during the early news hour I can ask a medical question of a local cardiologist (who will probably just tell me to check with my doctor), a lawyer, or civil servant. I can find out how to keep my floors from squeaking, or what to do if a business refuses to give me a refund for defective merchandise.

Younger generations, including boomers, whose lives are occupied with cars, computers, and the Internet, cell phones, pagers, and call-waiting, find little reason to turn to their elders for wisdom and insight. Their slowness dismays them. They don't know what to do with older people who aren't in the fray of life, rushing to and fro as they are. Some don't know how to sit and visit with a parent or grandparent, let alone just sit with them, if there isn't some activity connected with the visit like watching a video or eating barbecued steak.

Older adults bemoan the loss of connection with younger generations. Their own support systems may not be close at hand with children far away. The older generation's moral, spiritual, and cultural role has been lost because too little is expected of them. Empowering of elders to share their wisdom (knowledge gained over time in the skills of living) by presence and word is an important task but difficult. In a thoroughly secularized world it is hard for an elder to introduce words that describe how divine grace carries one through a difficult time without sounding pious, when the conversation is mostly about baseball scores and vacation plans. Yet a brief word about God's love at the prompting of the Holy Spirit can carry meaning for decades. He or she may never know the impact on the child.

This older generation knows more than any other age-group about dealing with loss and suffering, about hurt and forgiveness, about betrayal and faithfulness. When new retirees are not incorporated into church structures, some tell themselves: "I've earned my retirement. I've contributed. I've sacrificed. Now I'm entitled to a monthly check, to play, to travel." Yet the kingdom of God has too few workers to excuse some because of retirement or too many birthdays. The shopping mall, travel, or golf, do not answer the big questions of life.

I have mentioned often my mother-in-law, a tiny gray-haired woman, who could speak little English. I could speak little German. She had brought 12 children into the world in difficult times. Yet she conveyed God's care to me. I was facing the birth of my first child, far away from my own mother, and unsure of myself as I walked through this new territory of becoming a mother. On one occasion she said simply, "The Lord helps at such times." I don't know what incident in her life she was thinking about. Giving birth to her first child on an ocean liner in a tiny cabin, unable to speak the language, far away from family and friends? The death of a baby girl from summer diarrhea?

I carried those few words in my heart throughout four pregnancies. Such life-sustaining words do not come out of artificial piety but an intrinsic authenticity and
(continued)

Spiritual growth stands still unless there is deliberate forward movement.

At one time the elders were known as the sages, the prophets, the counselors, the wise ones, terms seldom heard today. Now they are often people left to their own devices following retirement until they come to the point in their lives that a younger generation, usually their children, steps in to take care of them. What their spiritual and emotional state may be is less important than making sure Mama or Papa is safe and secure in some institution.

As I watch this disregard of elders' wisdom, I ask: Does Christianity have validity when you are eighty or ninety? Only those older than I am can tell me. Is life meaningful when death is near? On Memorial Day, at the cemetery, I met a former friend, now in a wheelchair, age 95, who told me, "As long as I have the Lord with me, I am fine." Only the elderly can assure a younger generation that God's grace continues to the end. But I felt comforted that her son, well into his sixties, was pushing the wheelchair. She had him by her side also.

She affirmed her faith to me. We reminisced briefly about the time our lives had intermingled. Young and old bond when the elders are allowed to share an insight about life. I saw myself in my aging friend in another twenty years. I accept that I "image" the Christian life as an elder for those younger than I am. Elders are the only models of the mature Christian in the evening of life the young have. But if there is little or no interaction between the two groups, how can the young look ahead with joy and courage to the declining years?

knowledge of God's power. But it is hard to share such words of faith when the young person is preoccupied with a video game and loud music blaring in the background.

Why have older adults lost their wisdom roles?

Devaluation of wisdom. A big reason for the loss of roles is the discounting of wisdom as a necessary ingredient for life. There is lots of information floating around, but not much wisdom, which Theodore Roszak defines as "examined experience." People can spout without hesitation the winners of the last ten major football bowl games, or the number of miles to the gallon popular cars get. A wise person may know none of this and still be wise.

Wisdom teaching in the Old Testament was vigorously taught, usually by an older man to a group of young men, for "the glory of young men is their strength," of old men their experience (Prov. 20:29). Gray hair was a crown of glory (Prov. 16:31), not something to be camouflaged. The teacher in Proverbs didn't try to prove some syllogism, but forcefully asserted the truth and authority of tradition. The young scholars were urged to choose, especially regarding practical life issues— friends, use of alcohol, spending money, and how to meet temptations. Don't get too old before you get smart, the teacher admonished. Their teaching was reinforced by the desire to please God and be loved by their Creator.

Old Testament wisdom teaching gave ordinary people great freedom, for they didn't need to make a decision each time they were confronted with a moral decision. They had internalized teachings about the spending of money, binge drinking, carousing with loose women, or letting words fly from their mouths indiscriminately.

However, such direct wisdom teaching also incorporated a danger, for it could lead to a closed mind, as in the case of Job's friends. These men had firmly accepted that all punishments and rewards were meted out only in this world; there was no other answer to Job's dilemma than that he had sinned. His suffering was the direct punishment for some sin. They omitted an important component of wisdom—that to be a wise person requires one to evaluate each situation.

Shirley Yoder Showalter, president of Goshen College, Goshen, Indiana, writes in *She Hath Done a Good Thing* that "wisdom certainly will not prevent tragedy, pain, or depression. What contact with wisdom brings us is the conviction that the separations in our lives, no matter how deep, can be healed. . . . Wisdom also helps us within a time-bound world to see the things that will last."

King Solomon, writer of some of the proverbs, asked for wisdom from God at the time of his crowning. He had great intelligence (1 Kings 10:1-9). The Queen of Sheba exclaimed: "The half has not been told." He had great skills. He was a songwriter, botanist, biologist, and builder. He also had the keen insights into the skills of living that Showalter describes. Two mothers brought a child to him that both claimed. Solomon was able to identify the real mother through his insights into their natures. He knew which mother's love would last. These judgment skills, knowing good from evil, gave him a reputation in all the land.

The apostle James asks, "Who is wise and understanding among you? Let him show it by his good life, by deeds done in the humility that comes from wisdom" (Jas. 3:13). Elders should not feel they've got to be spouting witty one-liners they've memorized about life at every contact. In the Old Testament a wise person was one who trusted in the Lord (Prov. 3:5-6), who had self-discipline, who was not swayed by popular opinion, and who showed wisdom through a good life, not just words.

The greatest gift of wisdom is the example of someone who has learned the art of living. In our day it means the elder is not swayed by the advertising and media hype to indulge in stocking their shelves and closets with unessential ballast. The wise elder does not yield to peer pressure to look like their younger generations. A wise elder sets goals, is able to delay gratification, and uses time wisely. A wise elder recognizes the temptations to take shortcuts to the desired goals and chooses the better way. He or she knows the fear of God and lives by the teachings of Christ.

But that isn't all. A wise person has insight beyond the obvious into relationships (1 Kings 3:9) and justice concerns (Prov. 8:13). He or she is able to make difficult decisions for a group but also about personal matters. For elders today, that means knowing when it is time to quit driving or to move into a smaller apartment before children or physician pressure them to make changes. It is knowing the best expenditure of money in the afternoon of life. It is recognizing how important it is to get rid of the clutter in one's household but also in one's inner life. It is knowing when it is time to harvest one's life and hand over the fruit of the harvest to the young in the form of a life story. These are wisdom calls.

Wise men and women are those who spend time with God's Word. James encourages his readers to ask (call) for wisdom (insight) and to look (search) for it (Jas. 1:5). What will this searching for wisdom look like? Wise men and women aren't afraid to read material that challenges their thinking and forces them to look at both sides of an issue. They are people who pray and, especially, who take time to reflect on life and the ways of God with humanity. They avoid groups or organizations where superficiality is the norm. Above all, they have self-confidence to recognize their own wisdom but use humility in dispensing it.

Fast advance of technology. I met an older woman buying sewing notions in the store. "I don't know how to sew any more," she commented. I felt the same way. Though I know how to run a sewing machine, I haven't kept up with new sewing techniques demanded by new fabrics, computerized sewing machines, and new clothing styles. Without the technical training that children and grandchildren receive beginning in kindergarten, the older person's experiential knowledge seems outdated and quaint, writes Erik Erikson.

Consequently, I don't expect my children and grandchildren to come to me for sewing tips or cooking advice. They can get this much better from home lifestyle magazines. Likewise sons and daughters don't come to their elders for advice on farming by computer.

They go to county agricultural agents and the Internet to give them up-to-date agro-economic information.

The pattern not to seek advice from elders in technical areas consequently shifts to young people not seeking their advice in more value-laden areas. Lack of technical knowledge is confused with lack of knowledge about life because in this day the computer reigns.

What difference would it make if career and marriage counseling for the young were done with couples present who had spent 40 to 50 years together? Or if young entrepreneurs planning to start a business heard from someone who had managed a business for 40 years or more even if it wasn't in the field of technology? Some elders would be hesitant to offer their wisdom, because they haven't discovered how wise they are. Nobody's listening to them; or even asking for it.

Retirement signifies closure. Another reason the elders have lost their main role in church and society as wisdom-bringers is that retirement in our culture signifies a closure to and sometimes retreat from remunerative work and often from other responsibilities. With retirement some people feel like "has-beens" and are treated as such. J. Winfield Fretz, former college administrator and professor, writes in *Young or Old*: "At one moment, nothing was done without my consent; at the next, everything was done without consulting me." For a short time he found retirement uncomfortable.

Many retirees welcome the end of working days, and no one should be denied rest or a change, but healthy retirees should remain actively involved in life, including the church, not merely looking for ways to keep themselves busy. Elder wealth lies not only in bank accounts (and they are the demographic group in our society with the most discretionary income), but in their

I asked the manager of a local popular travel agency that plans motor coach tours to a wide variety of places in the United States and Canada, what percentage of his business came from older adults. I had heard it was 75 percent for this type of business. He shook his head vigorously. "Much, much higher percentage," he said. "At least 95 percent." His answer told me that older adults have discretionary income, time, and energy and are looking for new experiences.

contribution to worship, to service, to the conduct of congregational business, to the well-being of environmental and global concerns, and especially to life values by sharing their wisdom. Those are treasures worth looking for and should not be set aside out of fear of being bored by an older speaker.

At my first elder retreat several years ago, the group totaling about one hundred people, enjoyed 24 hours of great stuff—inspirational devotionals extremely well presented, stories that kept us riveted to our seats though we'd missed naptime, and entertainment that rivaled Jay Leno. But the church as a whole wasn't there to enjoy this invigorating experience. Youth and middle-aged were not hearing how elders can laugh together.

"Feeling retired by society, unneeded, and unproductive, [elders] cast about for some comfortable way to 'spend' whatever money and time they have in the years they have left," writes Erikson. He sees this loss of visible function on the part of elders as a tragedy, for old age is valuable in and of itself. The truth of aging is denied the young generation if the elders are seen only as active tourists, tennis players, shoppers, golf enthusiasts, and backpackers. As sociologist Dwight Roth says, "Their strong face of aging," which has been theirs throughout history, is gone. The young people are prevented from seeing life through their special vision when there is little contact.

Busyness of our age. Other reasons for the loss of wisdom roles include the busyness of our age on the part of children, parents, and grandparents. Children have athletic events and music lessons in addition to school and church activities, which increase in number each year, and dominate the calendar. The grandparents have volunteer activities, enrichment learning, and exercise classes which increasingly fill their days. Who has time to get together often?

Family living arrangements. Many grandparents live in small apartments in retirement centers. Some no longer drive, especially at night. Front porches with swings inviting children to come and sit a while are gone. Close contact, especially touching of other people's children, is discouraged in today's phobia about sexual harassment. Furthermore, there just isn't space or energy to play a game of catch or even to have a family dinner. To haul the china dinner set from its storage place, to clean the apartment, and find enough chairs is sometimes a monumental task. Yet something gets lost when the family gathering is transferred to a restaurant and fifteen people try to talk to one another in a noisy public place. Smaller families have meant fewer grandchildren to relate to. Some grandchildren in blended families spend the holidays with the noncustodial spouse.

Loss of grandparenthood. Another big reason for this loss of wisdom roles is the loss of grandparenthood as a distinct role in our culture. The former grandparenting traditions have fled, especially grandparents living close to or with their children in the same household. In many families grandparents once held an important role in caring for the grandchildren. But that is no longer true when young grandparents are still working or traveling. Also, not all older people want the role of grandparent. Some feel exploited when expected to look after grandchildren week in and week out. Some get minimal satisfaction out of childcare when bones creak and their own interests and needs demand attention.

In Japan grandparents customarily live in and raise children while parents work. Today this culture also suffers from the loss of closeness to grandparents when a job takes parents to another area. Then, closer older people are hired to become foster grandparents.

Lynette Wiebe of Winnipeg writes in the book *Young or Old* about the four-generation household in which she lives: she and her family, parents, grandparents, and a great-grandparent. She extols the extra measure of love and support each generation can give the other. Friends say incredulously, "How can you stand living with your parents?" Inwardly she responded, "How can you stand living without them?"

A group of Lorraine Avenue Mennonite Church members in Wichita, purchased an empty school building and land near the church, with the goal to build intergenerational housing on the site. The energizers behind the project, Willard and Ellen Ebersole, have built a duplex together with their children in which each family has separate living space but share the basement area. Other duplexes are in the process of construction.

According to Erikson, the older adults' task is to deal with the issue of generativity (devoting time and energy to the nurturing of the next generation). The alternative, he says, is stagnation caused by being fully absorbed in one's own life and pleasure. As we grow older most people (but not all) tend to mellow and values change. What they valued highly at age 50 and clung to with the tenacity of a pit bull terrier now at seventy is easily discarded. Objects like furniture, dishes, and books, dragged around from one place of residence to another, suddenly become ballast. Most of what the older generation had planned to do during their lifetime has been done or is now out of the question because of health or other factors. So grandparents have a choice—to find satisfaction in their own personal goals or to move outside themselves toward grandchildren and other people's children.

Lack of grandparenting models. Elders lack models of aging in this new age of elders and must blunder ahead. Similarly, today's grandparents lack models of grandparenting to match the cultural changes in children/grandparenting roles. Children and grandchildren often live far away, families have blended in many new configurations. A parent may be missing for several reasons: death, divorce, job demands, imprisonment, and military service. A grandparent may be absent for the same reasons.

The public image of grandparents has changed. At one time grandparents were recognized as those who passed on values, standards, and beliefs. The former image was of a gray-haired couple living on the farm nestled in the woods, whom you visited at Thanksgiving and Christmas. "Over the meadow and through the woods to Grandma's house we go" has changed to "Over the clouds and through the sky to Grandma's house we fly." And sometimes the young child flies alone without parents.

Decades ago this omega generation had few interests outside the immediate family. Nowadays grandparents are active in many fields of interest. Some even play romantic leads in movies and dramas—and in their own lives. And great-grandparents have moved into the picture, adding another factor.

Grandparenting used to be taken for granted. The roles and responsibilities of grandparents remained the same from generation to generation. Today's grandparents feel confused. How can they make contact with their grandchildren when infants get placed in child care almost at birth until they begin in school, or live far away? Society, including the church, condones divorce and also the uprooting of families to take positions miles away. Legally, they don't always have visitation rights after divorce when the children are in the custody of the in-law parent. Some grandparents feel deprived of their grandchildren.

How can older adults have more positive roles?

By being intentional. Roth suggests that whatever approach is taken to return elders to the role of wisdom bringers, it must be intentional. In an unpublished address he says, "We intentionally look for ways of bringing all of God's generations together in worship, service, play, meals, and prayers."

Through wisdom centers. Theodore Roszak argues that there is no dearth of wisdom. In an interview posted on the Internet by AARP, Roszak suggests that the problem is that no one is listening to the wisdom of the elders. There is no demand for their wisdom. When people today have a problem, they turn to a panel of experts—economists, sociologists, engineers, and technicians.

Roth advocates establishing wisdom centers in congregations staffed by elders. These would be similar to the Handyman's volunteer service available in many congregations for those who need a leaking faucet fixed or the lawn mowed. A wisdom center would make available elders in specialized areas, such as counseling, foster grandparenting, or family financial planning. The names of these elders and their areas of interest or expertise would be made known to the congregation.

Wisdom centers have their origin in what in early Hebrew times was called the village circle. This was the time for sharing information, exchanging ideas, telling stories, and learning truths. The village circle might be under a big tree (Judg. 4:5) or at the village well, or maybe at the open place by the large gate. Attendance was not compulsory but almost everyone wanted to come to enjoy the company, the stories, the songs, and the exchange of wise words.

Such wisdom centers in congregations would create opportunities to hear how elders confront their own aging. It would enable younger generations to learn firsthand what old means. It may be a surprise to some to know that older people's digestive system can't handle pizza at midnight, or several cups of coffee late at night, that caring for an infant or even a toddler all day is wearying, that there comes a time when preparing a big meal for the whole family is too much.

But such intergenerational involvement would also show that being old means having a sense of humor, a readiness to serve as one is able, a bottomless well of information about early church practices and values, how he or she dealt with temptations to drink or yield to sexual urges when in high school. And it would be an opportunity to see aging from the standpoint of God's power, not as loss of power or rights and strength, but rather, as Leland Harder writes in *Young or Old*, "as fullness of days and continuing sense of purpose."

Using Worldwide Web to help young and old to build community could be adapted to the church world if someone would keep touting the benefits of such electronic interaction. Don Isaac, professor of business and economics at Tabor College, in Hillsboro, Kansas, is one such defender of Web-based discussion groups. Students who otherwise won't say a word in class openly participate in Web-based courses. They feel less intimidated and more accepted.

He asks, "Is this community? Well, it's not quite like Sunday night at the Bergens' house, but it's also not just a collection of individuals." He adds that "community is simply gathering together with others to ask, 'What does it mean for us to follow Christ together?' It requires lots of time, lots of talking, and many deliberate acts of caring and sharing. Nothing will quite replace a hug, but in an era when nuclear

(continued)

A modern wisdom center looks commendable on paper but might be difficult to arrange and promote in today's world, especially where the church members don't know one another well enough to trust each other with personal questions. Work, athletics, church life, social activities, and even favorite television programs interfere. The sheer logistics of such centers look formidable. But here is another solution.

Through electronic wisdom centers. The increasing use of electronic media makes possible another type of wisdom center for the exchange of intergenerational wisdom contacts across the miles. A British organization has set up electronic mail facilities for up to 100 schools in the United Kingdom and abroad. Most are special schools. All cater to children who have some mental or physical difficulty with communicating.

Some of their projects include a "panel of elders" of many nations that answer questions, or grandparents who write their memories of the 1940s, for example. Another project makes possible that famous authors of bygone years through contemporary elder scholars answer questions about the original author's books. In the church world a central office could set up the Website and list names of people who agree to be elders.

or church families are scattered, more and more people will use the Internet to establish and maintain supportive relationships."
—Christian Leader, April 1999

Elders are the strength of the church in terms of attendance and moral and financial support. They're the ones who go steady with the church. They don't just make an occasional date. They're not likely to change affiliation when the church program no longer meets their needs. They should be keepers, not something tossed when a new trend hits the church. To set them aside is the same as tossing the accumulated wisdom of hundreds of years into the trash. A whole library is lost when an elder dies.

By intentional grandparenting. Such intentionality includes grandparents telling stories about their own childhood:

Stories about struggling to maintain sexual and moral integrity, courtship practices, heroism, and scary skeletons in the family closet.

Stories about what foods they enjoyed and which they despised. I hated gooseberry mousse, a sickly-looking pale-green fruit soup. I loved large Russian blintzes, lots of them. I tell my grandchildren this.

Jean-Paul Sartre wrote, "I could make my grandmother go into raptures of joy just by being hungry." My children did the same for my mother. She loved to feed them, for they ate everything she made, especially ethnic foods, but in today's overfed world that prefers hamburgers and pizza to homemade food, a meal of chicken noodle soup and an ice-cream cone is not always an invitation to bonding. Add to this the new factor that each person may eat only specific foods according to their chosen diet, and meals together can be a trial for the cook.

What should grandparents teach? Baking family favorites, whittling, a foreign language, sewing, fishing, whistling, reciting poetry, telling a joke, playing checkers, and whatever else they are skilled in, and sometimes not very skilled in. The main point is to spend time together. Be where the children are. Support youth activities. Help Sunday school teachers. Bake cookies for vacation Bible school and stick around to watch the action. Learn the names of six children. Send an e-mail to a child, including grandchildren, for no reason at all. Talk to the babysitter on the way home.

"It starts here," said Peter Benson, a nationally recognized child development expert. "We have forgotten where the power is. We have forgotten our own power, as human beings . . . to affect the lives of children." In a public address in Wichita he said that ours is "the most age-segregated society that has ever existed in the history of human civilization. Adults are not showing up in the lives of our youth."

How should they communicate? By any and every means of communication at their disposal: phone, videos, visits, audiocassette, fax, e-mail, letters and cards, photos, and money.

A man in his eighties told me he had bought a small

e-mail device with a keyboard and tiny monitor that made it possible to send electronic messages. He was as excited as a child with a new toy. In a matter of a few weeks he had received forty messages from children, grandchildren, and others. A whole new world had opened up to him. The monthly rate was relatively inexpensive, but he had taken the plunge into the computer world. It made him feel good.

What should they model? The joy of being alive. An interest in the world politically, economically, socially, and religiously by attending enrichment and/or credit classes, by showing patience, courage, and bravery in illness or dealing with the losses of aging, including death and dying. Humor is a great asset. An interest in the church and its mission through regular attendance and participation in its programs as the person is able.

A grandparent gives grandchildren a close-up look at how to age and an alternative to the socially emphasized stereotypes of aging. Role models should include all elderly, not just those who, according to societal thinking, are aging "successfully," meaning being fully active, charging ahead like a racer out of the blocks at the shot of the gun, running marathons at 80.

People like political activist Susan B. Anthony, conductor Artur Rubenstein, and physicist Albert Schweitzer are often held up as the goal for older adults to emulate. These people achieved tremendous creative works in old age, but they were exceptional human beings in early life and their unusual storehouse of creativity was not released with the onset of old age. Even these, eventually, had to slow down. The better role models are ordinary people, who struggle with arthritis, who overcome open-heart surgery, who sometimes struggle with depression, who discover gifts in themselves they didn't know they had as their years grow in number.

Grandparents as encouragers. Elders, particularly grandparents, should be encouragers, cheerleaders, hope-bringers, people who keep saying to the young, "You can do it. Go for it. You can be a Christ-follower." They give lots of praise, rare disapproval, and encourage commitment, faithfulness to promises, and honesty. Sometimes they become wish-granters. They do not belittle or criticize.

They tap the shoulders of those they perceive as being future leaders of the church and invite them to consider the call of God in their lives. One of the four top reasons why young people in the Mennonite church do not flock to church vocations is lack of encouragement to consider the pastorate. The Samuel Project conducted in the last year with the support of the Mennonite Board of Education was intended to tell why and how youth respond to the call of God and the church to serve as pastors. John A. Esau, reporting for the Samuel Project in the *Mennonite Weekly Review*, writes: "The lack of intentional encouragement is one of the constants across the data. The other one is the sentiment that such encouragement is needed and can be effective."

These older saints are life veterans. They've read the whole book, not just one chapter. They've got a perspective on life. They haven't aged to perfection, but they've got experience. They know what doesn't work. They have endured the changes, losses, and joys of decades of family burdens, church conflict and successes, and cultural changes. To ask their advice brings continuity to the generations. If we don't ask our elders for their reflections on their life experience, we are saying to them and to ourselves that living the Christian life for 40, 50, or 60 years does not really teach anything.

To set their wisdom aside in congregational decision making tells them and especially the young that all of this did not really require courage and faith. Or that having achieved 70, 80, or more years is a passive process ending in a product like a turnip which you can disregard if you don't like turnips.

Now try this:

1. Do elders need formalized courses in aging and grandparenting beforehand? Learning to grow old as one is growing old is not always sufficient, for the degree to which elders are involved in their own aging is determined by the degree of self-motivation, which sometime slackens as life becomes thin. To strengthen their motivation they need the encouragement of others. How can younger generations be encouraged to become involved in learning about their own aging?

2. Donna Froese, husband Don Schrag, and sons Sam and Joseph Schrag of Wichita often work together at ministry projects. When it is her turn to cook for the weekly church supper, they join her in the kitchen. As a family they mowed the church lawn for years. When I broke an ankle she came with her sons to clean the yard. They help in the church nursery and also in the Mennonite Housing "Paint-the-Town" project. High school senior Sam accompanied his father to Honduras to help with rebuilding following the hurricane.

   I asked Donna how she managed to keep them helping. She laughed and said, "Oh, I'm very firm." Then she added, "They were expected to help from the time they were young." There are murmurings at times, but the boys usually turn up at the next project willingly and cheerfully. Television watching is not a prime activity in their home. Reading is.

Another family took their toddlers along one morning a week to deliver Meals on Wheels. "That was the only life they knew, so they just assumed it was what every family did," said the mother. These children grew up volunteering to church and community activities. How can the church encourage more intergenerational service?

3. Each one teach one. Plan for a teaching evening when everyone comes prepared to teach a person of another generation, one on one, whether they are boomers, young adults, youth, or children. Youth can teach the older ones how to use a computer, to program a VCR, or how to watch a football game. Older women can teach how to make traditional foods, lap quilt, crochet, or embroider. Older men and women can share their knowledge of the history of community or church, or professional expertise. Children can teach older adults how to make items out of folded paper. A six-year-old grandchild once taught me how to make a box with a cover. Elders can teach children how to make a kite. Boomers can teach their parents driving tips.

4. Have elders write proverbs out of their own lives patterned after those in Proverbs. Look for someone in your congregation who can teach Proverbs enthusiastically. Publish these homespun proverbs in the church newsletter or weekly bulletin. I had a group of elders write proverbs out of their lives in a class focusing on their own wisdom.

> *Better is the older man who has reason to get up in the morning than he who sleeps all day.*

*There are three things that are too amazing for me,
four that I do not understand: the wisdom of the
body to heal itself, the peace of God that passes
understanding even when you are old, frail, and
alone; why a Kansas sunset is still beautiful after
seeing it for 70 or 80 years; and the love of a man
and a woman for each other after 60 years of
marriage.*

Any background book on proverbs will help with
structure.

5. Have children and young people identify wise elders in the congregation and then interview them
   about their life experiences and write a short report.
   In this way people who were born in the early
   decades of the twentieth century connect with people born in the 1980s and 90s.
6. Have someone teach a course in wisdom literature in
   the Bible. This includes Proverbs, Ecclesiastes, Job,
   some psalms, and parts of other books. How much of
   this is directed toward young people? To older people?
7. Plan for "Tuesdays with Morrie" events, in which
   children come with their questions to be answered
   by grandparents.
8. Have a small group of people plan four or five youth
   and family events for the year that include children,
   parents, grandparents—everyone. Make the youth
   service project an all-church event. In planning make
   sure that once everyone has come, the event doesn't
   end up with age-segregated groups as usual. Have
   plans to keep the age groups mixed.

Chapter 6

Respect in the Presence of Elders

*At Mount Sinai the younger generation of Israelites
was given a specific commandment with regard to
their parents—to honor them.*

Several years ago I was dropped off at the home where
I was going to be hosted for a weekend speaking
engagement. My hostess had not arrived home from
work. One by one her three adolescent and preadoles-
cent sons arrived home. As I waited in the living room,
each one walked into the room, introduced himself, and
greeted me. That little event made a lasting impression
on me. Those boys had been taught to be present to an
older person, even if they didn't know her.

A college student was planning to take part in a
school-sponsored mission trip. His tour leader advised
him to leave behind his earrings because some people,
especially adults, in the new culture might find them
offensive. "But everyone is doing it!" he replied. Some
things are best left behind as an experiment in youthful
indulgences when you are witnessing to another culture,
replied his leader. The young man rose to the challenge.
He placed his witness for Christ above his own desires.

Earlier I said that one task of the church was to
emphasize the role of elders as wisdom bringers.
Another equally important task is to encourage youth to

develop a stronger positive public image of themselves as disciples of Christ. Society has pushed them into a stage of life when going to school, maybe earning a little money to buy their own CDs and gas, and figuring out how to have fun times is all that is expected of them. How the young treat their elders is part of this revised image.

In one high school in Wichita, where I live, the school was in disarray. Teachers were leaving. Parents were pulling their students out. Grades were down, and the number of fights was up.

According to a newspaper report, the new principal introduced a program that has turned the situation around. It is based on respect—of self, teachers and staff, fellow students, and the building. Years ago we might have used the term "honor." "Respect" works just as well. One of the teachers said, "These kids are our future, and if you teach them to kick each other around and not have respect for each other, then this world is gone—you give up on the world," he said. "Teach them how to care and respect."

The apostle Paul admonishes Timothy not to let anyone look down on him because he is young (1 Tim. 4:12). He was to respect himself. He was to treat older men as fathers and younger men as brothers, older women as mothers and younger women as sisters (1 Tim. 5:1-2). He was to give "proper recognition" to widows. The King James translates this as to give "honor" to widows. His attitude toward his elders and also his peers was an important factor in his witness for Christ. That would offset any disparagement of his youthfulness. "Boys will be boys" was not to be an excuse for his behavior.

When I was young, every child memorized the Ten Commandments and the verses in which Ephesians echoes the fifth commandment:

"Honor your father and your mother, so that you may live long in the land the Lord your God is giving you" (Exod. 20:12).

"Children, obey your parents in the Lord, for this is right. Honor your father and mother—which is the first commandment with a promise—that it may go well with you and that you may enjoy long life on the earth" (Eph. 6:1-3).

Parents hoped these verses would come to mind at the appropriate moment and change behavior. I used the Exodus passage once in a sermon. A middle-aged woman charged down the aisle after the service to tell me the commandment to honor parents is irrelevant today, because parents neglect their children, often abuse them. Parents desert their children both in body and spirit to pursue their own interests. Parents are not always models to be honored. I had to admit there was some truth in what she said, but I wasn't ready to throw out this commandment. To honor unworthy parents is an act of grace.

What does it mean to honor, or respect, someone?

"To honor" is an unused term today but a common biblical and literary one. In the Bible and in literature, particularly English literature, husbands were expected to honor, or esteem, their wives; wives were to honor their husbands. Men were expected to maintain high regard for women. Many lynchings in the Southern states were caused by white men outraged because they thought black men had dishonored, or demeaned, their women, sometimes simply by looking at them. The book of Romans asks that all citizens honor the king and all rulers. Younger people are to honor their elders, children their parents, and believers the widows in their midst.

In medieval times the herald's role was to look after

matters that affected the dignity and honor of kings, noblemen, and gentlemen. Their right to honor was displayed by crests and coats of arms and by the pomp and ceremony that accompanied crownings, royal weddings, and funerals. Many a duel was fought between knights over the honor of a woman who had been insulted by one of them. A man willingly gave his life for the honor of king and country.

Many of Shakespeare's famous plays employ the theme of honor. One's honor was a cherished possession, not to be besmirched. Yet the well-known Sir John Falstaff mocks honor in *Henry IV*. He asks "What is it? A word." In King Lear the flawed king believes that the love and honor of his three daughters can be measured by extravagant words of filial loyalty. When the two older daughters utter the right words to the question who loves him most, he gives them the country, but they later throw him out of the kingdom. His youngest daughter who answers him that she cannot "heave her heart into her mouth," declares her love in simple words, but is disowned by him. He wants lavish praise.

Honor in the Bible. The term "honor" is not used as frequently in newer Bible translations as it was in the King James version, possibly because our culture has less use for the term than it had then. It is variously translated as splendor, dignity, and glory. As a verb it means to have noble purposes, to give respect or prominence to. Leviticus 19:32 admonishes the young to rise in the presence of elders. The opposite of "to honor" is to despise, sometimes to curse. In our day it would probably mean to be prejudiced against, or to look down upon with disdain or disregard.

Our schools have honors courses for those students able to do more and better work, especially on their own. In former marriage vows, bride and groom promised to love and honor their spouse. A women's honor, or respect, was considered destroyed when she was sexually violated. Such women were considered as "damaged goods" and not eligible for marriage.

In Arthur Miller's famous play *Death of a Salesman*, the main character, Willy Loman, is a traveling salesman (drummer) on his way down and out in a changing economy. He becomes discouraged. He is without sales prospects, without money, without a job, and hesitates to tell his wife that he has hit the bottom of the barrel. His whole career seems to be ending in a black hole. He contemplates suicide.

His faithful wife, aware of his failings, yet unaware of his betrayals of their marriage, in her much quoted speech, scolds her two young adult sons indifferent to their father's plight: "Attention, attention must be finally paid to such a person. . . . He's your father and you pay him that respect." She demands the two sons honor their father because he is their father. He failed them at many points but he was still always concerned about them.

We respect parents when we show interest in their lives, when we encourage and support them. There is enough in their own lives as the years add up to knock them down and allow self-doubt to enter.

We respect our elders most when we become their friends, and recognize them as people who want to hold and be held. They need affirmation, not more chiding for their sometimes grim rigid theology that condemns those they don't agree with. They need to be honored for their own sake, not for high and lofty opinions.

Honor, or respect, does not mean to treat nicely, to take out to eat on Mother's or Father's Day, or to send an appropriate card with nicely worded sentiment. Mother

Teresa honored the sick and indigent at her community house, Missionaries of Charity. She treated people with gentleness and reverence recognizing that even the man found in the street and overrun by maggots was made in God's image and needed respect.

Respect does not mean just being civil or even politically correct, as Richard Mouw points out in his book *Uncommon Decency*. He describes civility as "public politeness," or an external show of good manners. Mrs. Loman wanted more than that of her sons for their father. She wanted them to treat him with gentleness and reverence because she knew he was at the end of his resources.

We respect another person when we recognize that each person is patterned after God's image and within reach of divine grace.

Respect has at its core having compassionate convictions that that other person is someone God loves. It excludes elder abuse, road rage, refusing to pay one's bills, cheating on a test, gossiping about a friend, and even remaining seated when an older person enters the room, and especially leaving a parent to his or her own resources because they no longer are interesting persons to talk to.

Today's one-line put downs, which pollute most sitcoms, do not lead to honoring or uplifting the other person. We respect one another when we refrain from using demeaning language.

Biblical background. At the time the Israelites received the Ten Commandments, three months had passed since they left the slavery of Egypt. Memory of the Exodus and the passage through the Red Sea on dry ground was still fresh in their minds. Babes in arms fell silent as the long lineup of Israelites, mute, frightened, trudged through the riverbed. Little children would have clung close to their parents as they watched with terror the wall of water threatening them on each side. Parents looked only ahead to the shoreline, not at the backed-up waters. Freedom lay ahead. God had provided this safe passage out of Egypt.

The commandment to honor parents given to the Israelites at the stopping point at Mount Sinai states a relationship existed between children, their parents, and the land: "Honor your father and your mother, so that you may live long in the land the Lord your God is giving you" (Exod. 20:12). The commandment implies, "You lost the land I gave you once. You may lose it again if you don't honor your parents."

We understand more clearly what should happen between young and old if we know why the Israelites originally lost the land of Canaan. Jacob had twelve sons. The ten older brothers were jealous of Joseph, the eleventh son. They lost their respect for the family unit and sold Joseph, Jacob's favorite son, to the Ishmaelites who sold him to Potiphar, an official in Pharaoh's court. They broke the family unit to serve their own interests.

During a famine Jacob and his whole extended family traveled to Egypt from Canaan where Joseph, now an official in Pharaoh's government, took care of their needs. But here they were gradually forced into slavery. As slaves they lost their identity with father Abraham. The Bible has no written record of what happened during those four hundred years in Egypt, no story of walking with God. The 400 years of the Israelites in a foreign land are a blank. The only image we have of those years is harsh slavery with the cruel whip of the Egyptian overseer driving the overworked Israelites.

Then the Israelites returned to Canaan, their homeland, a land lost to them for these 400 years. In the fifth commandment, the Lord implies, "If you love the land more than your parents, you will lose the land again." These parents were witnesses of the Exodus from Egypt, God's miraculous deliverance from centuries-long slavery. If the children continued to witness to the story of God's redemption, they would keep both land and parents. Relationships with God and family were to be placed ahead of land and money.

I think of these sons of Jacob who sold their brother Joseph into slavery for twenty shekels of silver whenever I hear of children going after their parents' savings and estate before it is used up in long-term nursing care. The older brothers didn't want a relationship with their younger brother. Adult children want their parents' money; they don't want a relationship with the aging parents themselves.

Parents fight in the courts as to who will have custody of the children following a divorce. I have yet to hear of children fighting in the courts as to who will have custody of elderly parents unless there is money attached to the caregiving. At the stopping point at Mount Sinai the younger generation of Israelites was given a specific commandment with regard to their parents—to honor them.

The book of Esther is an interesting study of the rise and fall of someone who wanted to be honored by the king. As the fortunes of Haman, the ambitious Agagite, rose, so the fortunes of the Jews fell. But the resolution reverses their places. Mordecai, Esther's uncle, is honored, or lifted up, by the king, and Haman is dishonored and hanged.

Jesus becomes the guest of honor in Luke 14:1-14 in the home of a wealthy Pharisee. All sorts of people invited him to their homes, some to honor him, some to honor themselves by having an important teacher of the law in their midst. Protocol in seating at such an affair was as important then as it is now. The most important guests were seated at the head table to give them prominence. Jesus suggests that when invited to a feast, guests choose the lowest place, so that the host will not have to displace them when a more important guest arrives. "For everyone who exalts himself will be humbled, and he who humbles himself will be exalted."

Why should younger generations honor their elders?

Not mainly for biological reasons. At a Mother's Day celebration the emcee handed out roses to mothers. One mother received a rose as the producer of the most offspring. I chuckled to myself. We honor cows for being good breeders, not mothers. Having large families is not the best reason to honor parents. How those many children, by birth or adoption, are nurtured is a better reason.

Not for their greater righteousness. The elders are not to be honored because they have greater righteousness. Some parents are great models of right living, some are not. The example of less than perfect parents in the Old Testament runs to a long list:

To save his skin Abraham passed his wife Sarai off as his sister when they traveled to Egypt to get food during a famine (Gen. 12:10-20).

Jacob, father of nations, could be called an outright shyster for his many shady acts. He deceived his father, pretending to be his brother Esau; he deceived his uncle Laban when he sorted the flock to get his share (Gen. 27—32).

Laban deceived his nephew Jacob by passing off his daughter Leah as Jacob's beloved Rachel (Gen. 29:15-30).

King David didn't need a *Playboy* magazine center-fold to entice him to seduce the lovely Bathsheba (2 Sam. 11). Not all adults are models of behavior yet they deserve respect and honor.

Not for their abundance of gifts. Elders are not to be honored because they are lavish in handing over money and goods such as cars and watches, tickets to ball games, and new clothes to children and grandchildren. Yet often parents and grandparents are coddled for only this reason.

The younger generation is to honor their elders because the family is a special kind of bond in God's economy. It is not just an economic unit for income tax purposes, or to make life easier with two or more to do laundry, cooking, lawn mowing, and car maintenance. This bond is a spiritual one.

This commandment points to something special, something we may have lost sight of in the present-day furor over human rights.

Rabbi Abraham Heschel writes that the real bond between two generations is not a blood relationship but the "insights they share, the moment of inner experience in which they meet." They have discovered some spiritual truth together. He writes that the role of the father in the Old Testament was to lead children through moments of worship before God. He was expected to create the moment of spiritual awareness. He was to become the catalyst for the bonding experience.

Part of the Jewish family experience since the Exodus has been sharing the story of God's role in the Exodus in a ritual at the Passover meal. The youngest child asks "What do these things mean?" Then the magnificent story of the Exodus is told.

I have pondered Heschel's statement often. It is easy

My mother was the parent in our home who read the Bible and prayed with us five children at breakfast. My father had gone to work much, much earlier. Was my father's influence therefore negligible? He taught me in story and action that you can't control the working of the Spirit in people's lives. The message came through in bits and pieces as he told us about his early spiritual development and how people, including religious leaders, had tried to control the Spirit by making him jump through meaningless religious hoops.

As I have explained in The Storekeeper's Daughter, *later on, when he was in his 80s and he and I were visiting in my parents' small living room, he preached for me his sermon based on John 3:7-8: "You should not be surprised at my saying, 'You must be born again.' The wind blows wherever it*

(continued)

to speak about what we believe to our children. It is harder to convey our commitment so that they understand what it means to be a disciple, a follower of Christ, with their hearts. Sometimes this moment of spiritual insight happens during a family devotional, maybe at a special celebration, but I think it takes place more often as young and old relate to one another in all settings.

I realize the temptations of the young to take advantage of an older person's weaknesses of body and spirit are not new. They occurred already in Genesis. Jacob took advantage of his father Isaac's weak eyesight to deceive him into thinking he was his brother Esau (Gen. 27). King Rehoboam rejected the advice of the elders who had served his father Solomon during his lifetime and were now without political power. Instead, he listened to the young men who had grown up with him and were serving him (2 Chron. 10).

Yes, children are a nuisance because, young or old, they may encroach on parents' schedules. Older parents are a nuisance and burden because they expect some of their adult children's time. At Christmas, the most common request is "Don't give me things I don't need. Please, just give me a few minutes of your time." If older adults have the challenge to accept stronger positive roles related to the younger generation, the younger generation has a responsibility to honor their elders.

Spiritual bonding occurs when we intentionally keep telling ourselves in every way possible that we belong together—old and young—the essence of respect. We show respect for our elders when we interact together as a covenant community. Yet programs, particularly in large congregations, are often slanted toward families with children and young people. A church is considered incomplete or not a full-service church without programs for this age-group. The prevailing view is, "If it's for young people, I'm all for it." Yet those over age 60 should have as much programming and encouragement to keep grow-

pleases. You hear its sound, but you cannot tell where it comes from or where it is going. So it is with everyone born of the Spirit."

The truths of this sermon came out of his personal experience as a miller's son in the Ukraine, well-acquainted with the vagaries of the wind. He knew the sermon as well in his 80s as when he had preached it in his 20s as a deacon/evangelist in the villages on the steppes of south Russia. He had internalized the truth that the Spirit needs freedom to work. As he passed that truth on to me, we bonded. He understood me when I opposed the building of institutions before the building of relationships. I honored him for his commitment to the truth of Scripture and not to formulas.

One of Dwight Roth's students at Hesston College, Chad King, was enrolled in a class in which students visited older adults about one hour a week as part of "grandparent adoption." Many of these elders are quite frail. Chad wrote:

I love old people. I saw past Adolph's elderly body and glimpsed, through his eyes, the spirit of a beautiful soul. We talked an hour about Christianity. We had talked about these things before, but today I saw the man's soul shine through his eyes. He was talking most of the time, but today I was sitting in silence admiring a soul, grown stronger by God's love and many years of perseverance in faith. It was cool!

We started our conversation about singing and expressing one's faith. We discussed the way a person witnesses by the way he behaves, his character. He told me the story of his

(continued)

ing spiritually as the younger ones. They have unique spiritual needs in the evening of life. The church honors this group when it does that.

An ancient Chinese Taoist story is told about a master carpenter and his apprentice who were looking at an old, gnarled tree. The older man asked the younger one, "Do you know why this tree is so big and older?"

"No," said the apprentice.

"Because it is useless. If it had been useful, it would have been cut down, sawed, and used for furniture. But because it is useless, it has been allowed to grow. That is why it is now so great you can rest in its shade."

When the value of the tree is its usefulness, it is cut down and used for lumber. When the value of the tree becomes the tree itself, it is free to grow in the light and provide shade for tired wayfarers.

When the value of "elderly" becomes the persons themselves, all who are younger will find encouragement, wisdom, and comfort by their presence.

Surely, the generations have mutual roles that need to be revived.

Now try this:

1. How were older adults honored (respected) when you were a child? In some cultures schoolchildren always rose when the teacher entered the room. Why haven't those practices been maintained?

2. Why has the practice of undercutting with a quip or a jibe caught hold so firmly in our culture? Does watching sitcoms and late-night talk shows have a role in popularizing put downs and lessening respect for others?

3. Is a certain type of attire, hairdo, and posture necessary to show honor to God when attending church services?

4. Elder abuse is becoming prominent in the news. Adult children not only neglect their parents, but steal money from them and even physically harm them. How can the church help?

experiences in Africa with a person from England who was an atheist. Adolph's life made a man believe in God simply because he tried to show this atheist God's life. I want my life to be that much of a testimony to God's greatness and love.

The strength of Adolph's faith struck me. It's huge. I asked him to pray for one of my friends who is struggling with faith in God. He promised me that he would, and I know that his prayers will release an entire airborne division of angels to effect change in my friend's life. I believe he has that much spiritual clout.

Chad's story is a wonderful example of a young person honoring an elder by spending time with him. (Used by permission)

5. How do young people see the role of grandparents in their lives? What would they like to see happen?
6. Discuss what would empower elders to pass on their wisdom to younger generations.
7. In communities with growing retirement centers, nearby churches are experiencing a rapid increase in the number of elders attending. Brainstorm how you would deal with a sudden increase of 70 to 100 elders in your congregation.

Chapter 7

Reinvent Your Life at Any Age

We are witnessing the dissolution of the linear life plan, a change that will vastly affect the way generations relate.

My father was born in 1896 in the Ukraine. At that time his life journey had very clear stages modeled for him by his elders. He knew from experience that when you no longer went to the fields every morning because your age had caught up with you, you sat on the bench in front of your whitewashed house and visited with your neighbors passing on the street.

For as long as I can remember, his store in the little Russian immigrant village in Canada where we lived had a couple of benches in front for the old men of the village to sit and visit. That was the way things were done. That was the role of elders in the villages in the Ukraine. The practice had been brought over with these Russians and Ukrainians to the new country. Life was a one-way street, down which you moved from one life stage to the next, ending in death. This linear view of life was held by many similar cultures.

A linear life plan was important when the average length of life was short. At the turn of the century people were considered old at 50 or 60. Life expectancy was less than 50. When you were finished with one stage, you eased to the next.

Shakespeare describes these life stages as seven in number, beginning with the "mewling and puking infant" followed by the "whining schoolboy." The final stage is second childhood when the person ends "sans teeth, sans eyes, sans taste, sans everything." A dismal view of life.

Another description of this end stage can be found in Ecclesiastes 12, where the preacher describes this time as "the days of trouble." He says, "I find no pleasure in them."

Fortunately, my father lived to be 91, but, unfortunately, he lived rigidly in step with the life stage theory. He didn't know that you could reinvent your life at any stage. (By life stage I mean a developmental period of life during which people face similar problems and thus have similar perspectives.) He and my mother brought us children up with the same lockstep life stage view.

After childhood and schooling, came job preparation, followed by marriage, parenthood, middle age, and old age. You lived according to what was age appropriate and in sequential order. Getting married before you had a means of livelihood was frowned upon. Few thought of going to school after age 30 or 40.

Choices were for life. The big question for children when I was young was, "What do you want to be when you grow up?" No one ever asked, "What do you want to be like when you are old?" Early in life you chose or were directed to a career, sometimes already in high school, and stuck with it even though later on, you hated your choice. Often circumstances did not make it easy to switch careers, even jobs. During the Depression years you worked at whatever was available, even digging ditches, to keep bread on the table.

My father chose to be a storekeeper, a vocation that

began with a period of apprenticeship in the Ukraine in Russia, followed by the opportunity to manage a small store for a company in Canada. Marriage, family, and civic and church responsibilities were fitted in at the appropriate times. At age 70, he retired and waited for death, not in a morbid sense but with the satisfied knowledge that his life journey was nearly over. His main contribution to life had been made. He never considered that death might be several decades away and that these decades also had to be lived meaningfully.

People who live their lives by this rigid life stage plan hesitate to ask themselves: "Is it too late at 40 to begin medical school or adopt a child?" or "How about a new career when I am 65?" Such people are kept in place by their own assumptions about where they are in the life cycle and also by the government, which says retirement age is 65 to 67. The first half of life consists of climbing the ladder in their chosen profession. Academic learning and even character growth is taken care of in youth. With retirement you start climbing down the ladder, letting go of responsibilities, positions, dreams and goals, and new learnings.

Traditional life stages. Linear thinking about adult development means predictable sequences of learning, marrying, working, raising a family, leading, and succeeding. Anything that slows or sidetracks progress in personal life is not welcome. Everything is orderly and with planned change. The focus is on progress beginning with the potential of youth, which is expected to develop and unfold.

In linear thinking youth are portrayed romantically, high on a pedestal. Who hasn't heard the phrase, "I'm willing to do anything if it's for our youth"? The idea seems to be they have supreme value because the future of the church depends on them. They haven't ruined their lives as yet.

Elders are seen as having less value because they're moving downhill and have made their contribution to life, a perception that causes some to have low self-esteem. It never feels good to know that you are part of the group that is on the way out. Being psychologically edged out keeps elders looking back on that successful career with little motivation to keep moving ahead.

Omitted in this kind of linear life stage thinking is the demographic fact that in the 21st century (2030) there will be about 70 million older persons, more than twice their number in 1996. People over 65 represent almost 13 percent of the population in the year 2000 but are projected to represent 20 percent by 2030 (AARP 1997 statistics). Church membership can often count at least 10 to 15 percent more older adults than a sampling of the general population. That means the church of 2030 may have 30 to 35 percent older adults. Some congregations will have even more, up to 40 and 50 percent. The church's future depends on its older adults as much as its youth. They are also the future of the church.

Why do numbers matter? I've sometimes said that it makes a difference whether you have one cat in the house or ten cats. Numbers make a difference. The larger the number of elders, the more they can influence cultural values about aging. The larger their number the more important it is that they model Christian discipleship to the young in both close encounters and through their public image.

The linear life plan is not for everyone. Ken Dychtwald and Joe Flower in *Age Wave* state that we are presently "witnessing the dissolution of the traditional linear life plan," a change that will vastly affect the way the generations relate because all ages may be engaged in the same activity at the same time. Going to school, for example, may be an activity young, middle-aged, and old are engaged in.

Erik Erikson, whose seminal work in developmental psychology of adults has strongly influenced the life stage theory, describes the life course as a series of psychological tasks. Every individual has natural and cultural responsibilities that arise during a certain period of a person's life that must be faced and dealt with before going on to the next stage. He or she is socialized to act in ways appropriate to each successive role: teenager, student, parent, worker, civic and church contributor, and retiree.

According to Erikson, each of these life stages has conflicting tendencies. For the older adult the polarities are generativity versus stagnation. Through concern for the welfare of the future generation, or generativity, elders find a sense of meaning in life. If this generativity does not take place, they stagnate and life becomes empty.

Today certain transitions are less tied to a certain age or stage. Degree completion programs during adulthood, many years removed from college, are becoming popular. Parenthood, once a role for young marrieds, now is put off for later to the 30s and even early 40s. Theorists today see life as a more flexible passage, a cyclical journey.

When life expectancy was limited to retirement age or less than a decade after retirement, the life stage theory worked well. It was important to get age-related tasks done, for there was no second chance. Death ended many dreams.

Now that many people live to age 80 and 90 and beyond (the age-group over 85 is the fastest growing demographic group), the life stage theory has weaknesses. Demographics have changed the face of aging. Today elders generally face a prolonged period of life in which they are relatively healthy and energetic but lack a recognized role in the economic and social life of society.

This is equally true in the church. Some older adults live an ambiguous life for possibly 20 or 30 years after retirement, as many years as they worked, asking "What is my role?" The church offers no significant roles, and is often overjoyed when the older members withdraw from leadership roles to the sidelines.

Other trends. Dychtwald and Flower see a number of trends occurring in our world: the development of more adult-only housing; the rise of AARP, the national organization for older Americans; health care focused on older groups; the decline of youth-oriented organizations such as Boy Scouts of America; and an increase in the number of books on aging with intergenerational concerns (care of aging parents, grandparenting, and so forth).

Dychtwald and Flower also see the nuclear family as disappearing. Up to the middle of the 20th century the patriarchal family was dominant with two generations alive at one time. Elders were few in number. Children abundant. The median age was 17.

The nuclear family with two parents and one or two children at its core began about the 1960s. Elders were increasing in number and children decreasing. The median age was 29.4.

Today the nuclear family is being replaced by the matrix family, or adult-centered family, with relationships primarily between adults. The median age in 1988 was 32. The adult-centered family is transgenerational with a number of generations in the same household bound together by friendship and choice as well as by blood and obligation. Today each grandparent has only half as many grandchildren as in 1950 and each child has twice as many grandparents as a generation ago.

A new mystique. Elders may live 20 to 30 years with the ambiguity of unclear roles in church and society, not always sure what the discomfort is they feel about their stage in life. In 1963 feminist Betty Friedan wrote about *The Feminine Mystique,* an unnamed discomfort housewives were feeling with their role in life. It seemed to be limited to cleaning and polishing what was already clean and polished. Housewives were encouraged to fill the void in their lives with shopping and ornamental display of their femininity. They felt perplexed about their role in life.

Susan Faludi in her recent controversial book *Stiffed: The Betrayal of the Modern Man* argues that men in our modern world are going through this same turmoil. Stripped of their connections to the wider world and also invited to fill the void in their lives with consumption and a "gym-bred display of . . . ultramasculinity," they are experiencing a masculine mystique. They wonder what they're here for. Not all readers agree with her premise.

Elders are encouraged by our culture to jump the traces that held them to the work world as soon as chronological age allows them to. They are urged by the example of their peers as well as advertising to fill their lives with travel experiences and retain a personal trainer to keep their bodies in shape. I am convinced that some are experiencing an "age-related mystique." Some elders recognize this is a culturally-induced mystique and consequently search for more significant ways to fill their days, not that new experiences and exercise are unimportant. They challenge the culture that sends them into retirement and navel-gazing. Boomers are predicted to change the face of the aging even more as they have changed everything else they have connected with in their journey.

I see the "Aging Mystique" as the unnamed discomfort of retirees who, after the initial thrill of self-chosen leisure has worn off, wonder what role God has for them. They feel frustrated when they look for significant roles in the church and society. They are told their main task is now to volunteer at something, at anything. They have the ability to make major decisions, but not the opportunity. Though they may have managed a work force of 100s in their place of business and were responsible for a budget of several million, dumbing down to putting labels on letters seems a little thin, despite preaching that the good Christian is humble enough to do any job. Not all in this group are challenged to find a volunteer task that fits their skills and gifts. Some were weary of responsibility and are ready for lesser roles.

The busy ethic. Consequently, some retirees turn to what David J. Ekerst calls "the busy ethic." It derives from the work ethic, which identifies work with virtue. He asks, "What do people do with a work ethic when they no longer work?" They work at keeping visibly busy, which legitimates the leisure of retirement. I've heard countless retirees say, "I'm busier than when I was working." This busyness includes part-time jobs, volunteering, grandchildren, maintenance around the house, hobbies, pastimes, socializing, much of it good stuff. Conversation about retirement focuses on "What occupies your time?" not "What gives meaning to your life?"

Frederic M. Hudson in *The Adult Years* writes that much current literature on adult development is written with the assumption that order in a person's life should be predominant over change, yet older adults live in a period when change is predominant over order.

Adults today have multiple options at transition points in their lives and random opportunities to move in new directions. They don't need to be tied to the linear life stage plan. Personal responsibilities change. All adults are invited to participate in lifelong learning experiences. My daily newspaper lists an abundance of workshops and learning experiences in multitudinous areas. Throughout the life cycle today, "adults keep rearranging the same basic life issues (such as identity, achievement, intimacy, play and creativity, search for meaning, and contribution) around changing perspectives that our personal development, aging and social conditions evoke from us," states Hudson.

Cyclic life view. Hudson further explains the cyclic view of life as going in circles with repetition of familiar patterns but with different meanings to those patterns at different times. At age twenty a young man may have accepted a job to earn money to go to school. At 50 he may accept a new job to fulfill a lifelong dream of working with environmental concerns. Life tasks are repeatable in different ways.

Learning a new skill is not limited to one period of life. Life develops through change. Life makes sense in good times and bad, in growth and decline. Continuous learning is essential for reeducation, renewal, and redirection. Gone is the thinking that when you are retired, learning ends. The cyclic view admits to both the good and bad in aging with gradual physical losses but an enriched inner life. The cyclic view sees every life period as meaningful and valuable. I heard a retired lawyer say recently that he wanted to die at the height of his spiritual strength, not when it was at low ebb. For him that meant to keep climbing.

Changing the way we think about the life process

At the same time as elders are reinventing their lives, young people can also begin marching to the beat of a different drummer. They don't need to fall in line with becoming the "typical teenager." As I've already mentioned, teenagers were invented in the early 1950s as a distinct age-group with certain psychological and social characteristics. The concept of a "youth culture" was born following the Depression and World War II, writes Wendy Murray Zoba. An extra abundance of young people came crashing on the scene with "free time, extra money, and energy to burn. Football teams, cheerleaders, bobby socks, and jukeboxes all came together to create a new 'youth culture.'"

With them came the "youth rally," an attempt to bring an alternative to worldly entertainment into the church world. Youth work had an emphasis on entertainment, she writes. I recall at the zenith of Youth for Christ rallies while I was attending a Bible college in Winnipeg, Canada, some of our church school leaders were hesitant to endorse this grand scheme of "Christian" entertainment to draw young people to Christ. But we young people went anyway. It was wonderful.

Like the term "teenager," the terms "young adult" and "middle age" are also fairly new constructs but ones which are extending their later boundaries. Young adults can be well into their 30s, and as long as they are young adults, the church knows not to expect much of them. Middle age which once began at 40 or 50 now extends to the 60s. And the media report that another new age-group is growing rapidly: the tweens, youngsters between the ages of nine and 14, with already tremendous buying power and control over their lives, although this is debatable.

Zoba writes about the "hand-off philosophy" in youth ministry. The junior high youth group is "handed off " to the senior high group. The problem of assimilation comes after senior high. Who do you hand them off to then? George Barna, in his book *Generation Next*, notes that there is a marked drop-off rate in church attendance once young people graduate from high school. They tread water until after marriage and having children.

Looking at life through a lens that allows for more flexibility in life stages will not do away with teenagers treading water until they grow up, but will allow them to take on more responsibilities at an earlier age. Zoba quotes one youth pastor as asking himself, "Why am I doing this?" The youth were coming to church to be entertained and then going home to be entertained by television, music, and movies. It allowed them to become passive onlookers and reduced youth ministry to encouraging passivity and being just another consumer item.

Fewer models of youth ministry, according to Zoba, in her article "The Class of '00" in the February 3, 1997, issue of *Christianity Today*, focus on inner spiritual development. They give young people a chance to develop their soul. They allow them to grow up.

Do adults, especially elders, have a role in youth ministry? According to materials I checked, adults aren't always welcome in youth ministry for several reasons: they haven't the commitment of time and energy over the long haul, they can't handle the different styles of worship, and they aren't willing to consider a more revolutionary view of the gospel.

New wineskins for youth ministry. Zoba offers three new "wineskins" of youth ministry which do not surrender the gospel to consumerism. The first is "peer ministry," or kids ministering to kids. The emphasis is

Wendy Murray Zoba describes a Christian version of the Jewish tradition of bar mitzvah, a milestone in the life of a Jewish child, that one congregation introduced to bring the generations closer together. During the ceremony the child leads a substantial portion of the liturgy which includes the reading of psalms and chanting the Torah and Prophets. She explains that this special ceremony provides a meaningful ritual whereby the youth "is expected to master the practices and rites of community and commit himself or herself to the faith as an adult member."

I saw something similar practiced at Reba Place Fellowship in Chicago several years ago. At a boy's 12th birthday the church had a special celebration of affirmation, with liturgy and prayers, including circle dancing around the child.

A birthday is a good time to introduce

(continued)

on discovery and implementation of spiritual gifts of the youth for church leadership. "Teens reaching other teens create an atmosphere of trust and affirmation that enables young people who might not otherwise hear a gospel message to hear, and relate, and find release," writes Zoba.

The second model "celebrates the established church, while finding innovative ways to integrate young people into its tradition. Mentoring and discipleship groups are a big part of this model. Youth are encouraged to participate in many aspects of services, such as readers of Scripture, as ushers, or by sharing special music." Zoba quotes one youth leader as saying, "Sometimes when they read the Scripture they don't do a great job at reading, but their involvement says to them, 'This is your church, too.'"

The third model, which falls somewhere between the first two, has teen leaders of cell groups and an adult coach, or mentor, and regular teen-flavored worship services followed by joining the larger congregation for their worship service.

In all three types of ministries, teens are encouraged to live radically. They are assured they don't have to be grown up to be used by God. "We need to know what God wants us to do and begin now," states one contemporary music artist.

In the church, reinventing the teen years might mean cutting out some pizza parties, lock-ins, and asking those who

something like this or else baptism, in which the candidate(s) would have a significant part in the church service, in the reading of Scripture or liturgy, and a reading of his or her faith journey to this point. What about a similar celebratory effort to send retirees into their new life?

are Christians to join the adults in developing strategies for church growth and taking on leadership in various areas. Young people should see learning as something they will be doing a good part of their whole lives. Zoba states that in the twenty-first century youth will emerge as the new heroes of the same revolution that turned the world around 2,000 years ago. And if the youth are being challenged to live radically for Christ, shouldn't this be the challenge also to elders?

Ken Dychtwald in his newest book *Age Power* writes that living in the 21st century dominated by older adults, age 65 will no longer be a marker for retirement. I am convinced that in this new millennium "when I retire" will be an antiquated phrase. Retirement as we know it today will disappear as adults reinvent their lives, change careers, retrain for a new one, find new goals in Christian ministry and service. Adults will be challenged to be persons in motion, continually undergoing change. Adults will emerge as new heroes along with the youth to live radically for Christ.

Paul Tournier in *The Seasons of Life* writes, "If living

means choosing, and if in adulthood this is true to an even greater degree, then choosing becomes the supreme vocation of old age, when life has become privation and earthly treasures have lost their glitter." Choosing will be the habit in all areas of life from deciding not to have bacon at breakfast to consciously freeing oneself of the thought patterns and theological understandings of earlier life stages to be ready for what God has in mind for elders and their relationship to the other generations. Longer life will eliminate age restrictions for certain activities.

So the word is to haul both young and old back into the church. No sitting in corners waiting for parties or for life to end. Mix the generations. Because they have not been asked for their wisdom, help elders to recognize it and encourage them to share it. Help younger people to recognize their potential to accept more grown-up responsibilities than they are aware of. Every believer at any age is gifted and needed in the household of God. Discipleship is an invitation to all age-groups.

Now try this:

1. Plan an evening of singing with half the choruses those that the older generation sang in the 1940s and 1950s and half those that have moved onto the church scene in the last decade. How different are they?
2. Discuss the two theories of life development: linear and cyclical. Which one have the members of your group followed? What makes it difficult to change? Is it necessary to consider change?
3. Ask your youth leader to discuss his or her philosophy of youth ministry.
4. What are ways both old and young can feel greater ownership of the church as "my church"?

Chapter 8

Young and Old as the Prophetic Community

*Tragedy occurs when there are no dreamers among
the people of God.*

An ostrich escaped from a zoo and found her way to a
local barnyard where she laid an egg. A bantam hen
gathered her brood around the huge egg with the words,
"I just wanted you to see what can be done." She was
asking her chicks to dream big.

Yes, it is important to dream big. A production-consumption society places a high priority upon usefulness,
upon people who can perform useful tasks like bringing
food to church suppers, organizing major events, or
helping to paint the sanctuary. It sets a lesser value on
people who can no longer produce. Such societal values
set aside those people—the young and the frail elderly—
who cannot contribute much to the church in terms of
aggressive doing.

Therefore, the task of church leaders is to bring all
generations around the "egg" to show them the bigger
task that lies before the church, but which doesn't need
carpenter tools, kitchen equipment, or money. They
need to reintroduce elders to their task as dreamers for
Christ's kingdom and to the young their task to become
visionaries.

Robert K. Greenleaf writes in *Servant Leadership*, "Not

much happens without a dream. And for something great to happen, there must be a great dream. Behind every great achievement is a dreamer of great dreams. Much more than a dreamer is required to bring it to reality; but the dream must be there first." Part of the revised agenda for the old men (and women) is to dream the big dreams for the church, to be the prophetic community. Elders will be judged by the quality of the dreams they pass on, not just by their deeds.

Young and old will dream. Read again the passage in Joel which the apostle Peter refers to in his great Pentecost sermon about dreamers and visionaries.

> *In the last days, God says,*
> *I will pour out my Spirit on all people.*
> *Your sons and daughters will prophesy,*
> *your young men will see visions,*
> *your old men will dream dreams.*

> *Even on my servants, both men and women,*
> *I will pour out my Spirit in those days,*
> *and they will prophesy (Acts 2:17-18; Joel 2:28-29).*

The prophet Joel was speaking of a future time of spiritual renewal and restoration. God's Spirit would be poured, not just sprinkled meagerly, on all people, not just a few elect leaders. All servants of God would prophesy, or foretell, with no distinction of gender, age, or social class. With the Spirit would come all the charismatic gifts. People filled with the Spirit dream, or envision, the future to discover what wonderful new possibilities God has for the church of Jesus Christ.

South African leader Nelson Mandela spent several decades as a political prisoner but never gave up his dream for freedom for the black race. Jesse Jackson, African-American leader, told an audience in Wichita about his grandmother's funeral. At the coffin he touched her body. It was cold and lifeless. The realization came to him that dead people don't dream. He was concerned about his fellow African-Americans, dead in spirit, with no dream of freedom for their race. If you are alive, you will dream. And then you will push those dreams into reality.

The apostle Peter, in his great Pentecost sermon, was saying that Joel's vision was being fulfilled during his time. The Spirit had been poured out on all those gathered for the feast and would continue to be poured. Pentecost marked the coming of the Spirit.

The parts of this text that trouble me are the references to the old and young. They shall be part of the prophesying community through their visions and dreams. Some congregations feel relieved when stodgy elders are out of the system and the middle-aged are in the harness of church leadership. They dismiss the young as too inexperienced and therefore ineligible to speak the Word of the Lord to the entire congregation.

But tragedy occurs when there are no dreamers among the people of God—whether the dreamers are young, middle-aged, or old, and when the agenda is mostly business—how to pay for a new roof and when to have the Christmas program.

Dreamers, the prophetic voice of the church, often come from the underside of church life, from the powerless, the ones with the least to lose, the ones not always listened to. Elder dreamers are concerned with the future as the present will affect it. Like Joel's words, they may bring both a message of judgment of sin and grace.

Though older adults at some time may have to lay aside active leadership roles in the church, particularly in administration, their role as dreamers and prophets should never stop for retirement or a trip to Hawaii. Their task is to be cheerleaders at the sides of the playing court, encouraging, shouting, "Go girl! Go boy! You can do it! We're behind you!"

Prophetic dreaming. Visions and dreams were especially prophetic activity in the Old Testament. Walter Brueggeman in *The Prophetic Imagination* writes that "the task of prophetic ministry is to nurture, nourish, and evoke a consciousness and perception alternative to the consciousness and perception of the dominant culture around us." The task of prophets is to bring about an awareness that an alternative community is possible. This community "knows it is about different things in different ways."

Former missionary John Driver speaks of this alternative consciousness as the church being a contrast society to the dominant culture, which is how the Anabaptist community began. The early Anabaptists walked to the beat of a different drummer than what the state church ordained. They saw with enlightened eyes a different kind of community. All believers have a task, and that is to see with these enlightened eyes (Eph. 1:18) what is possible through the pouring forth of the Spirit. Dreamers are not envisioning a present reality but a yet invisible future of the church.

Some people might say that elders are poor candidates for dreaming. They're considered critical, strangers to passion and exaltation, beauty and wonder. Sometimes sexless and bloodless. Youth are the better candidates for dreaming with their zest for life and willingness to look daringly into the future.

The need for a prophetic imagination is frequently mentioned in writing about church life. Ronald Marstin in *Beyond Our Tribal Gods* states: "What determines the qualities of the societies we build if not the quality of the dreams we dream? As human beings we must dream. Without dreams there is no tomorrow, only despair and hopelessness." The older generation will be judged, for their paucity of dreams limits the next generation.

In *Enough Is Enough* John V. Taylor cites an interesting historical tale about how dreaming affected a whole society. In ancient Rome the economic system did some strange things over a period of time. In the first century a pound of gold was worth 1000 denarii. By 301 it had risen to 50,000 denarii and 36 years later to 20 million denarii. By 350 the price of a pound of gold was worth 350 million denarii. The Roman Empire fell. Why? Inflation or a deeper cause?

Taylor states that "A culture is an outward expression of the dreams by which the people live." He argues that the Roman Empire fell because the people had lost their high goals for themselves. They were living in the present. They didn't plan for the future because everything was going well.

Many early church institutions, such as our church-related high schools, colleges, and seminaries, began with the dream of a few concerned people that church schools could shape the lives of young people for Jesus Christ and his kingdom. Most congregations began with the dream or vision of some farsighted men and women that God's witness would blossom in that spot.

I listened last week to a group of people retell the story of the congregation in Wichita to which I belong. Nineteen charter members bought a rundown church building for $3,000 in the middle 1940s and committed themselves to being God's witness in that spot. Today about 630 people worship together as a result of that dream.

Ray M. Zuercher in his well-told history of Messiah Village in *To Have a Home: The Centennial History of Messiah Village,* begins his account with the story of two women of the Church of the Brethren in Christ, who in 1895 conversed about starting a home for old people. Unlike Martin Luther King Jr., they weren't gifted in lofty oratory like the famous "I Have a Dream" speech. But they could observe the needs about them and connected that observation to their Christian commitment. The result is Messiah Village, near Grantham, Pennsylvania, a community for older adults with more than seven hundred and forty residents.

The quality of the future of a congregation is determined by the quality of the dreams of its members. Without these dreams the congregation becomes spiritually anemic, much bothered by institutional details. Both the prophet Joel and the apostle Peter say this task belongs to both the elders and the young. And if we want today's young to be dreamers, the way for them to learn is by seeing this gift exercised in others and then to interweave their dreams with those of their elders.

By his example Jesus showed his followers how important it was to dream or to see beyond the present to a future reality. Jesus recognized the Pharisees as people without spiritual vision, blind to Christ's new patterns of living. They kept people tied to rules and regulations. They never saw what freedom from the letter of the law could do. Jesus came into their midst and said, "You don't need to live in life's worn-out patterns. There is another way, a way of grace. See what God has in store for you."

Christ saw in Peter, impulsive, headstrong, outspoken Peter, the rock on which his church would be built. He didn't put Mary into a box restricted by traditional women's roles. He saw her as a disciple, as a learner, and commissioned her to go tell his disciples that he had risen from the dead. He saw in the despised Zacchaeus a person in whom the Spirit of God could dwell. People with a dream see the possibilities of the church in our day and how all the members, young and old, can become part of that dream.

Dreams for the church today

In an opera about Joseph the dreamer, son of Jacob, one of the characters sings, "Any old dream will do." But that playwright was wrong. Not any old dream will do. What the church needs most today is visionaries, people who think God's thoughts and dream God's thoughts for the kingdom of God.

One life task of the young adult is to define his or her dream of adult accomplishment, to find a mentor to guide, to develop a vocation, and to open him or herself to new intimate relationships.

Elise Boulding, Quaker futurist, would add another task for Christian young adults. She said at a conference of church-related colleges several years ago, "Every student entering college should spend the first week working on visioning the kind of world Jesus envisioned and where they fit into it." In other words, they should spend the first week of college finding Christ's dream for the world: a world of love, peace, harmony, forgiveness, cooperation, and enough for all.

New retirees often spend the last years of their working life thinking about their plans for the future. These may include travel, hobbies, remodeling the home, reading, and just doing nothing. I propose that they should spend the first six months to a year of their retirement finding God's dream for themselves and the church and how they fit into that dream now that they have freedom from daily employment.

Paul's dream for the Ephesians was "that the eyes of

your heart may be enlightened in order that you may know the hope to which he has called you, the riches of his glorious inheritance in the saints, and his incomparably great power for us who believe" (Eph. 1:18-19).To dream God's dreams for the world means to see with new and different eyes—Spirit-enlightened eyes—what God's plan is for the mature adult.

What is God's dream? God had a vision of those who chose to follow his call to live in obedient covenant relationship with God and with one another. God called out a people for himself to glorify him. The Old Testament Hebrews caught this vision of shalom from time to time. It was a bigger idea than peace, or the absence of conflict, but the privilege of being a whole member of God's covenant community. Dreams that remain unconnected to life may simply die, and with the loss of dreams, the individual's sense of purpose.

At Kadesh Barnea the children of Israel came to a halt because they lost their dream. Ahead lay the Promised Land. They could enter it if they chose to. Twelve men went ahead to spy out the land and returned with their report. All agreed it was a land flowing with milk and honey. Caleb and Joshua were convinced it was God's Promised Land. The Lord was with them. They did not need to be afraid of what seemed like giants in the land. But the other ten spies were not convinced.

Why didn't the Israelites enter the Promised Land at this point? Because some among them, in fact, most among them, did not share the dream, the hope, the vision of living in God's land of plenty with enough for all. Because they refused to acknowledge the possibility of the dream of shalom in the Promised Land becoming reality, the Israelites were condemned to wandering in the wilderness for 40 years.

This event at the border of Canaan shows a sharp contrast between the young and the old generations. The old resisted forward movement. They had it all figured out. The obstacles were too great. Walter Brueggeman writes in *The Land*: "The older ones are characterized by calloused, calculated knowing, beset by quarrelsome impatience. The little ones who have no claim to power, leverage, or virtue, who are totally vulnerable, shall receive the promise. . . . The land will be given not to the tough presuming ones, but the vulnerable ones with no right to expect it."

In my mind's eye I see the Israelite families gathered around their campfires in the evening discussing the decision, their children sitting nearby hearing their parents speak their fears of the giants stalking the land in Canaan. The ridicule and disdain in the voices of their elders as they talk about their future is impossible for the little ones to shut out. Fear overcomes the hopes that had kept them going thus far. They let go of the dream of the Promised Land. As they wandered in the wilderness, one by one the older ones died off and only the young were left. No one over the age of 40 except for Caleb and Joshua entered Canaan 40 years later. What did they learn from this event? What can we learn from it?

To dream God's dreams is to have a clear idea of God's mind, thoughts, plans, and purposes of the richness and glory of the Christian community with the Holy Spirit as the energizing power. Change comes out of imagings of the future. This does not mean looking for strange lights in the sky, or articulating great ideals in vague and fuzzy terms.

What is the dream? What faith dreams should everyone be dreaming, particularly the elders who have more time for prayer, meditation, and listening before God? It means brainstorming together and alone what the

Christian community might look like 20 or 30 years from now if there were no obstacles. Action strategies come later. Here is part of my list:

> * *The possibility of men and women, young and old, finding redemption in Christ Jesus and living in relationship with God. God can make new creations out of flawed human beings.*

> * *Families once again as strong units with the marriage bond secure.*

> * *Individuals overcoming sinful behaviors and living in relationship with Christ.*

> * *Christians loving the unlovely people in our society and bringing them into equal relationships. Christians loving one another even if different in culture, race, and body image or physical condition.*

> * *All people finding justice, having enough to eat, and a place to live safely without threat of violence.*

> * *Young and old moving joyously, willingly, into the service of Christ.*

> * *The church as a strong vibrant body, moving ahead as an institution but also as spiritual body, daring to risk the giants in the cultural land, resisting society's addiction to consumer goods.*

Dreamers can only dream if the world makes moral sense, where not everything happens by chance, or where good and bad is dispensed by a whimsical God. A dream empowers a human being or a group.

A friend asked me what my dreams are regarding an intergenerational church? His question caught me off guard. I am old enough to be called an elder.

What is my dream as an elder in the church?

I dream best for my own congregation, an urban church of about 640 worshipers in a fast-growing suburb of the city. The parking lot is heavily dotted with the young family vehicles—minivans, or "suburban assault vehicles," as someone has called them, driven most often by young mothers as they sally forth to games, practices, church, school, and other kinds of activities. Young growing families are our church's strength as are the growing number of elders. Wichita is a good place to relocate in retirement with its wide variety of cultural events, services to older adults, and the ability to get anywhere in the city within 20 to 30 minutes. Another church asset is the large group of vigorous young people.

Programs that involve young and old are cropping up here and there: organized prayer support for youth, an annual brunch for older women sponsored by Mom's Carelink, a program linking young women with older women, an annual father/daughter dinner, and several others. But what else could be done?

My dream for my congregation? Let me make this wish list practical.

To know the names of at least ten of the young people sitting in the four or five rows of chairs at the front of the auditorium other than the ones with whom I have family connections. Maybe I'd even agree to just five. But the young disappear at the last amen like a drop of mercury on a slippery slide.

To have more of the younger adults, including middle-aged, stop to greet me and my friends in the halls

"Bringing down the age wall pays big dividends at transition points. The Bible doesn't have a word for teenager," notes Dennis Sawyer, senior pastor, of the Church by the Side of the Road in Seattle. He says that if parents come to him and ask, "What programs do you have for teenagers?" he smiles and says, "We have church. If everything for teens has to be specialized . . . how do you keep their faith alive when they graduate from high school or college, and all the folderol stops? You've conditioned them for beach trips and lock-ins, and suddenly they're disappointed. We believe it's better not to set teens up in the first place."
—Dean Merrill, "Not Married with Children," Christianity Today, July 4, 1997

and not keep their eyes strictly ahead of them, telling me indirectly, "I don't know you, so I don't need to talk to you."

To have regular elective study classes in which all age-groups feel comfortable and enjoy the interaction of old and young so that being together doesn't seem like an experiment in cross-cultural communication.

To be able to participate in worship services with a variety of ages and both genders participating, clearly showing the congregation each week an appreciation of all age-groups. Special youth worship services are great, but why not mix old and young on a regular basis?

To see young people stopping to ask the older woman waiting with her walker to be picked up and taken home how she's doing.

To see old and young, boomers and elders, singles and married, sitting together at church meals.

To have representation from all age-groups on all congregational boards. One pastor commented that his goal for years has been to have an age span for the governing board. They need not all be elected members. Some could be emeritus members.

To hear of older members mentoring younger people in close connections, not just praying for names of people they don't always know even by sight.

My thoughts get clearer as I continue. I would like to see a church in which age is referred to as little as possible in ministry programs and where young and old choose from the same menu of service and worship.

I would like to see youth ministering in as many different ways as they have gifts, including preaching on occasion, not just on Youth Sunday. I dream about the next generation and the strength and vigor they will bring to the work of the gospel.

I dream about opportunities for older generations to pass on their wisdom or common sense to the younger ones—the kind of wisdom that used to be shared around meals at home in intergenerational groups.

I would like to see post-high school and college young people finding the transition from the hoopla of youth groups easily and quickly—and comfortably— into the full life of the church instead of dropping out until they get married or wander off to some church that has an active singles group.

And I would like to see singles of all ages taken seriously.

Elders can transfer their dreams to the younger generations

I think back to the time when I was working in the city, a year out of high school. I joined a Sunday school class in prophecy, including dispensationalism, taught by a middle-aged man. It was not the usual Sunday school pap, but adult stuff that made me think. His dream was to give everyone his vision of apocalyptic times. Mr. Ediger treated us like adults old enough to make decisions of thought. I began to work out the meaning of my own encounter with God.

Since then I have discarded much of what I accepted so wholeheartedly at the time—the charts about premillennialism I could duplicate without thought, the detailed notes about the Daniel passages, and the much-paged issues of the *Prophecy* magazine I ordered. But I remember that he had a dream about the future of the church that he passionately taught to others. Dreams are only transferred to others when they are painted with passion, not the washed-out pastel colors of a beginning artist's still life.

The big issue I face in this book is how can young and old communicate when the gulf between them gets wider and deeper, especially in larger congregations where strong institutional organization is needed to manage programs? Intergenerational relationships become a minimal focus in congregations where population size makes close interaction difficult. It is easier to work with bodies of people of the same age.

Yet when old and young have connected, great things have happened. The great world missionary movement of 1886-87 began with young people, from farms mainly, who yearned for wholeness of life. Their lives were growing and broadening. The result was teams of young men and women who went all over to Africa, Asia, and Latin America to establish new colonies for the kingdom of heaven supported by the older generations.

Some ideas picked up in research and conversations:

Let Christ give you the dream. If we have no dreams and no visions, we are not responsive to the Spirit and we limit God. God is waiting for a partner in a young or old man or woman. That means spending time with God in the study of the Word, prayer, and being open to God's working in our lives through other people.

I have found that a dream begins with feelings of holy discontent or the awareness there has to be another way, a better way. It begins with a concern about mediocrity and loss of vitality in the Christian life and great sorrow that passivity or even big business is taking over the church. A dream begins with the uncomfortable feeling God wants something more.

Be aware that the prophets and dreamers can be the disturbers of church peace. To utter a dream for the church is to lament, a political act, calling attention to the fact that this is not the way things should be. What is happening is not right. Many of the psalms are laments, a crying to God for justice. They openly declare the evil of the present situation. The language is not prayer meeting language, but sometimes brazenly bold. The reader is aware that this pray-er is encountering God in a way difficult for him.

Old Testament prophets were sometimes asked to do some rather strange things. Similarly dreamers do not speak of blue cloudless skies and fields of fragrant flowers. They speak of things not all want to hear about—wholeness, freedom and justice, peace with God and with people. To accept someone's dream for the church means rearranging our inner thought life, and this can be uncomfortable.

People outside the centers of power in the church dream more because they see more objectively. But their dreams will not always be seen as a vision from God because they may disturb the peace and even flow of church life. Prophets today, young or old, are not seen as prophets but as meddlers.

Make yourself responsible for the dream God has given you. Obey the nudge. Embrace the dream. Make the dream yours. Tell others about it. Let the dream be so big you feel embarrassed to talk about it. It takes a lot of heart muscle to move a dream. Arthritis gets to our hearts as well as to our bones as we grow older. We are tempted to say, "We've done our share. Now it's someone else's turn."

Put your reputation on the line as you verbalize your dream and act on it. Give your dream away in church newsletters, in Bible classes, in casual conversation. Be a spokesman for the dream. Wrestle with the dream, work long and hard at it until you can reproduce for others what you are thinking and feeling about God's will for the church.

I have a dream about the role of elders in the life of the church. I keep writing and speaking about it. Some people look at me with incredulous expressions. Some say, "I'm too old for what you're talking about." Others affirm and commend. The dream becomes clearer. At times I yield to pressures that I am off the beaten path, and I step aside for a while. But then the Spirit nudges me once again. And I write this book.

Why elders as the dreamers?

In William Faulkner's short story, "The Bear," the small dog, a feisty little animal, dares to come before the huge bear and bark at him. The dog's utter powerlessness gives the small creature courage. It is scared but not afraid. That is a good way to describe the dreaming elders of our congregations. Scared but not afraid. They have little to lose and much to gain. And they know that they have fifty to sixty years on young people.

Many elders are powerless in the congregation, their

words being dismissed as out of sync with the times. The purpose of visionaries, prophets, and dreamers is to offer the church what God has given them and be ready to be rejected as the prophets were. Dreamers for God are willing to be misunderstood, to expose their inner thoughts, and become vulnerable to free others. Christ said to the disciples: Lay down your power as individuals and identify with me. I want no doormats but people who deliberately pick up my cross and follow me. Release your need to be in control, to push ahead and be on top. Let go.

Dreamers need a community. Mennonite Central Committee, the relief and development arm of the Mennonite and Brethren in Christ churches, developed out of a small group of dreamers buoyed up by a huge community of like-minded people. In the early 1920s they had a dream of being able to help their needy brothers and sisters in the famine-stricken land of the Ukraine. A group of like-minded people needs to be present to not let the dream thud to the ground. They help refine it and find a launching pad for it.

As a society we used to talk about what humans could do. That is no longer true. The big news story today is what computers can do. The newspaper carried a story this morning about a man who had decided not to leave his residence for one year to prove that all his needs could be met by ordering food, clothing, entertainment, and so forth by computer. The computer had become his god.

The real question for us is what can the Spirit of Christ do when poured on young and old? Without a dream, the elders lose a sense of responsibility to the church and to the age in which they live. They become comfortable as second-tier members.

Without a vision, the young fall in step with the call of contemporary culture to self-indulgence. Our daily newspaper carried the story of high school youth bothering merchants in one of our larger malls. A spokesman for the group said, "We're being pushed to turn to a life of crime and drugs, if you don't let us wander around the mall. There's nothing to do."

What was their problem? In part it was that they had no dream to lift themselves out of their miserable little world to see beyond today. They didn't see themselves at age 40 or even 70. They weren't dreamers. They never dreamed about the possibilities life has for them as God's creation. They were caught in a narrow rut.

God only gives visions to those who are looking for them. God doesn't bother people with a vision if they'd rather walk the mall or be a couch potato. One day the prophet Isaiah was in God's presence when God asked, "Who will go for me?" Isaiah could say, "Here am I, Lord. Send me," because he was within hearing distance. The challenge is to remain within hearing distance of God. Then God will give the dream for an intergenerational church.

Now try this:

1. Have the elders of the congregation spend a retreat day dreaming (brainstorming) about their congregation as if money, time, and energy were inexhaustible. Where would they like to see the congregation a year from now, five years from now, 25 years from now? Have them report to the congregation. Have the young adults do the same and then compare the visions.

   (Brainstorming has several principles: let the ideas flow as fast as possible, piggyback on another person's idea, consider no idea as too silly or outlandish, never judge a contribution during the brainstorming with a comment such as "That would never work." After the brainstorming session, refine and discuss your contributions and action strategies.)

2. The Jewish leaders of Jesus' time could only see the bits and pieces of the law, never the whole, never the wonder of a life redeemed by God. Jesus came to fulfill the law and help people see the whole of life when lived by the grace of God's truth. What are some areas of church life where we see only bits and pieces?

3. List some people in your congregation you would call dreamers. How are they regarded? Do they get opportunities to speak their dreams?

Chapter 9

Where Have All the Heroes Gone?

The choice of a hero, whether Mother Teresa or Elvis Presley, tells the world a lot about the person.

During the late 1950s and 1960s J. D. Salinger's *Catcher in the Rye* became many a young person's first "bible." I saw copies more worn with use than an octogenarian's Bible. This monologue by a 15-year-old school dropout dominated the young adult imagination. Holden Caulfield's teenage confession of doubt at the threshold of adult life launched the generation gap. It and similar literature denounced the adult world as empty and phony, not worth emulating. That generation gap was an all-out war between the young and their parents.

Young Holden wanted to preserve his innocence and keep children from entering the superficial world of adults who were interested only in how many miles you get to the gallon of gas. They laughed at movies that weren't funny. His boarding school cafeteria served steak only when the board members were present. Such hypocritical actions disgusted him. He saw nothing inspiring or beautiful in adults he knew. In the end he realized he couldn't keep children from growing up. Every person must be given the opportunity to reach for the Gold Ring and either hold onto it and succeed or fall.

The first time I read Salinger's *Catcher in the Rye*, the

long confessional monologue with its occasional vulgarisms turned me off. Yet because it had captured the minds and hearts of thousands of young people during the riotous 60s, I tried again to read it through their eyes. Holden was speaking for them. He was saying that young people had too few adult models. Materialism, phoniness, and superficiality had become the main characteristics of middle Americans. Too much was being done to maintain the image of respectability. Holden wanted naturalness, spontaneity, and beauty.

Other spokespersons of the times advised young adults never to trust anyone over the age of 30. Why the turnoff? Why the rage? In the church the young accused adults of sterile religious language, empty theology, and stilted action. Organization took precedence over organism. A believer's relationship with God was limited to the vertical dimension with a resulting social blindness.

A lack of heroes. At the bottom of Holden's problem was the fact that he had no heroes to look up to. He saw all adults as phonies, people who were consciously posing, not acting natural and sincere like a child. For him society, including religion, had provided no role models to be an authentic human being. He was unable to communicate with adults.

The disillusioned 50s. The 1950s began a period of supreme disillusionment despite the victory of the war. During World War II people had banded together with great zest and courage willing to die for their freedom, but they had never learned to band together to live. The 1950s were a period that couldn't risk any deviation from respectable and conformist behavior.

During this time "teenager" became firmly entrenched in our vocabularies; before it had been "schoolboy" or "schoolgirl" and "college man or woman." College students were addressed as Mr. and Miss. Professors were addressed by their titles and surnames. Mature men and women were called Mr., Mrs., and Miss.

The emphasis in the 1950s and 1960s was on bigness in all institutions, including the church, colleges, government, and business, with resulting depersonalization. The little people had to compromise themselves or move out. Whereas the Depression had made the essentials of life more important than superficial status symbols, the 1950s moved in the opposite direction.

Dietrich Bonhoeffer's *The Cost of Discipleship* was also popular reading among the more mature young persons because it promoted radical discipleship and rejected the idea of cheap grace. However, Shirley Nelson's *The Last Year of the War* moved too close to the truth for some as she revealed the Christian community's readiness to tamper at the edges of religious reality to make the church look good. Her novel had adult characters who pushed legalism in ethical issues to keep all young believers firmly within the fold.

Ernest Becker, as quoted in *Psychology as Religion* by Paul C. Vitz, wrote: "I think that today Christianity is in trouble not because its myths are dead, but because it does not offer its ideal of heroic sainthood as an immediate personal one to be lived by believers. In a perverse way, the churches have turned their backs on . . . the need to be something heroic in this world." In researching this topic, I found mention often of youth's lack of heroes but not what to do about it.

What is a hero? The term hero is seldom used because it is an outdated and quaint concept dating back to Greek mythology. Instead we have celebrities.

Literary critic Robert Penn Warren writes that "the hero is known for having achieved something, the celebrity is known for being known."

Daniel Boorstin in *The Image* adds that one of the oldest of human visions was "the flash of divinity" in great persons. The secret of their greatness was God's secret. The people of their generation were grateful to God for their greatness. He writes that two centuries ago when a great person appeared, people looked for God's purpose in that individual; today we look for his or her press agent.

"Our age has produced a new kind of eminence . . . the celebrity. The celebrity is a person who is known for his [or her] well-knownness. . . ." Celebrities are "neither good nor bad, great nor petty, made by all of us who willingly read about [them], who like to see [them] on television, who buy recordings of [their] voices."

Gerald Leinwand in *Heroism in America* sets the two apart even more. A hero is known for greatness of achievement brought about by a self-sacrificing spirit. Such a person touches the imagination and inspires movement. Unlike celebrities heroes don't boast about their prowess, yet must have witnesses and reporters if they are to live on in posterity. That's where the elders come in—to keep identifying and affirming the heroes in our midst to the young.

A hero is worthy of imitation because of greatness of achievement and self-sacrificing spirit. Heroes face a challenge and respond. Rosa Parks, the African-American woman whose refusal to give up her seat to a white man, launched the modern civil rights movement. Yet her heroic action didn't burst forth at the moment when she was on the bus. Her biography shows that her action was consistent with her character and behavior long before this.

On the other hand, the celebrity is someone who is instantly famous, created by publicity, writes Leinwand. Celebrities live for self, for the moment; ambition is their only real human quality. They promote consumerism. Often he or she, upon being "discovered" by some talent agent, bursts on the scene.

He adds that celebrities have raw, likable animal appetites and are accepted even if they rage against conventional behavior by a self-designed lifestyle. They live for the moment. Their driving ambition is their only real human quality. For them it is important to give the audience a sense of their complete control and adequacy at all times. The super-celebrity can be summed up in one phrase: "Hunger for power." Push ahead or be pushed out.

Not that young people do not choose heroes to worship. From 1980 to 1991 *World Almanac and Book of Facts* conducted an annual poll among America's youth asking them to identify their heroes. The winners included people like Burt Reynolds, Alan Alda, Sylvester Stallone, Michael Jackson, and Michael Jordan. All were from the field of entertainment and sports except for one woman, Paula Abdul, and H. Norman Schwartzkopf. None were elders.

I was disappointed when I asked a group of 70ish adults to speak about people who in their experience exhibited the traits of self-denial, courage, and daring in their Christian life; in other words, heroes. Few could point to such a person. I wondered why. The choice of hero, whether Mother Teresa or Elvis Presley, tells the world a lot about the person. Leaders of the faith look pale and insipid compared to someone who can score home runs time after time or make several million by acting in a few commercials or launching a top CD.

The task of elders is to help young people sort

through life and find their own heroes. The celebrities and the infamous will push to make themselves known. In an affluent, consumer age, in which the American values held forth are self-confidence, success and top performance, heroes of the faith have a hard time being noticed.

A wife who cares for an invalid husband for thirteen years without complaining doesn't get much press. Her battle is daily. Becoming well-known is not her goal. All she wants is sufficient grace to complete the tasks of the day. She competes against no one. An older man who has taught a young boys' Sunday school for more than forty years gets very much taken for granted because his faithfulness lacks a drive for control, or to be in the limelight. But both the wife and the Sunday school teacher are heroes.

The Christian faith is life-affirming, not attention-seeking. In its denunciation of sensuality, self-indulgence and hedonistic lifestyle, it may give the impression that the gospel doesn't want people to be happy. Harry Blamires in *The Christian Mind* points out that the religious community mistakenly attacks the young themselves rather than the institutions, such as the media, the entertainment and advertising world, that make money off the young by promoting hedonism. He argues that youth are basically romantic manifested in their sharpened sexuality and sense of joy in the arts, such as music and art.

He advocates that the church should help the young see life through the eyes of the artist, the poet, and not allow the inner richness of life "to be vaguely identified with the sins of the flesh." Young people need to be encouraged to paint, to compose, to write poetry and fiction, to fling their hearts to the stars and reach for something greater. The church's task is to lead them to heroes

If I pick out one hero from among the many I have known, it would be an institutional leader. The man had intended to be a missionary, but the circumstances of World War II prevented that, so he became the principal of a struggling Bible school in northern Saskatchewan where my husband was teaching. This man developed the trust of the constituency because of his clear faith in God and dream for Bible education for young people. He was therefore able to inspire the constituency to give money, time, and energy to build the institution.

His colleagues joked about his approach, even while they respected him. At first he'd say, "I think the Lord would have us build an auditorium (or other project)." Then when the project was launched and the money wasn't coming in, he'd say, "The reputation of the Lord will be hurt if we fall down on our giving and have outstanding debts." (continued)

who can draw their spirits to higher goals and help them hang onto their soul.

Christian celebrities. Today the church, young and old, is subconsciously drawn to an overidentification with big-name Christian personalities to attract people to the church. We have the feeling that Christian celebrities somehow connect the entire congregation. Everyone knows these people. They give church people someone to relate to.

Conference speakers must have a well-known name and, better still, a spectacular experience to talk about—such as a dramatic turn from "real sin" to the new life in Christ, with most of the speech devoted to the depths of sin. "Regular sin" doesn't cut it to draw a crowd. A former staff person of a large city congregation commented that those in charge of retreats were compelled to find better, flashier speakers so that people would turn out. An in-house speaker/teacher lacked appeal.

Some large Christian periodicals look for a Christian musician or popular speaker with celebrity status, and preferably good looks, to adorn their cover page to attract readers, sending out the message that the more popular you are, the stronger Christian you are.

In the church we de-emphasize hierarchy and authority, at least in spirit. The bishop system crumbled some time ago. Women are creeping into leadership roles. The roles of leaders have changed with pastors now chief administrators instead of being chief inspirer through word and life. We have congregations with strong executive-type personalities but not heroic self-sacrificing people. Hierarchy and authority are still with us in different form.

Congregations are more critical and cynical of their leaders and some do not see their pastor as a spiritual hero as much as a successful administrator. There is admiration for the organizers of great church plants who have strong personalities, exuding energy. Yet the leader's accompanying traits are not always depth of spirit and pastoral spirit as

Usually he was successful because he willingly made personal sacrifices for the school, and put his whole will, energies, and talents into his work. He provided a model of sacrifice, not fearing the obstacles. He was forthright in his preaching, but I often wondered if he wasn't a very lonely person. Outside his work with the school he had little to talk about. I believe Christ was honored most through his witness because of his strong faith, his willingness to act upon it, and his readiness to do whatever the situation demanded—whether it was digging a ditch, plumbing a house, chairing a meeting, or preaching a sermon.

some of the big Christian TV personalities have shown. Just as our culture breeds and discards celebrities, so congregations do the same, applauding a leader for a time, and then shifting to a new one when relationships sour. As a result we have also de-emphasized true heroes and mentors, which can come from the ranks.

Missionary heroes. Heroes exist in the eyes of those who admire them. Once we greatly admired, held high, those among us who dared to go to unknown countries to evangelize the "heathen." Any full-time Christian away from home had a certain glamour. A missionary report, especially with entertaining slides, brought out crowds because it gave the viewers a glimpse of heroic greatness. Someone had had faith to risk dangerous living conditions in a different culture.

Today we have demythologized our missionary heroes. When we didn't know what missionaries were experiencing in an overseas country, we had this vague but wonderful image of missionaries facing severe physical dangers such as poisonous snakes, angry lions, and fierce natives, that tested physical and mental acuity and spiritual courage. Legends of missionary prowess and escapes were born to be repeated in home congregations again and again. Many missionaries deserve praise for their willing sacrifice and readiness to serve in lowly difficult assignments year after year, sometimes without furlough. Every branch of the church can point to these heroes.

But today, with many church members traveling overseas and seeing for themselves that there are no snakes in a modern flush toilet, good food is generally available, and even ample recreation, the missionaries become ordinary Christians living in another country—except in areas of persecution.

Why the quest for authentic "saints"?

For one main reason: When younger generations recognize the true heroes in the congregation, they see Christ-followers who point beyond themselves to a greater One who has brought them forward in their life pilgrimage.

The Bible is full of heroes of the faith (Heb. 11). It confronts us not with general and abstract ideas but with men and women who are human and real. They were flawed creatures as we are. Sometimes they stumbled and fell. Other times they rose to great heights.

Yet it is the encounter with these heroes of the Bible that inspires readers to make commitments, to choose, to take a decisive stand. Young adults need not only encounters with the men and women of the Bible but also those heroes of our times who dare them to take sides, to shoulder responsibility, to make commitments. They need to see the Word of God lived out in flesh and blood.

Delbert Wiens of Fresno Pacific University writes that we still have profoundly Christian men and women among us. Wiens, in his "From the Village to the City," feels that we seem to have lost the capacity to recognize these godly men and women, and we fail to show our youth who they might be or to hint at the long road, the great travel that it takes to join their ranks. And so the young lose any truly profound sense of who Jesus Christ is. They are forced to image Jesus in the light of their celebrities, and he becomes a popular hero too, like "Jesus Christ, Superstar."

Wiens describes how his father helped him see an older man in the church as a hero. He identifies H. H. Flaming of Oklahoma as one who had a deep reverence for the exceeding greatness, power, holiness, justice, and judgments of God.

Wiens's father, H. R. Wiens, described Flaming to him. He never finished grade school but was always learning. He loved nature in all its forms. "At night he could point out the constellations and tell the myths connected with them. He was a homespun philosopher and great thinker, a lover of men, very practical, humble, and a great leader. He led in such a humble way that you never feared approaching him and never sensed at the moment that he was leading you. . . . Many times at conferences, after the theologians and professors had come to their wits' end, someone would turn to Brother Flaming and ask him what he thought. In his very humble way he would say, 'I think it would work this way. . . .' and it would work."

Wiens concludes, "I have not wholly forgiven my church for forgetting its H. H. Flamings while pointing to celebrities and organizers."

Why have the great heroes departed?

The spirit of sacrifice is gone. We as a church have lost the sacrificial spirit necessary for heroism. Christians fade into the cultural landscape like a rabbit in winter, yet Scriptures are full of people who kept risking because of their commitment to God. We sing "Dare to Be a Daniel," and retreat to our couch and remote control. As I read Christian literature the word "sacrifice," meaning giving away what might be needed for self, is seldom used. Yet it is a biblical concept beginning with the Old Testament altar sacrifices to Jesus' command to deny oneself, take up one's cross, and follow him (Mark 8:34). The secret is learning how to live life as an offering to God, not trying to see how comfortable we can make life for ourselves.

Mary sacrificed her reputation by sitting at the feet of Jesus, an action unacceptable for women; Peter, the apostle who received the vision of creeping and crawling things and was told to eat, sacrificed his loyalty to Jewish tradition and dared to cross the threshold of a Gentile. Was he scared when he did that? Probably, but he still stepped over.

It is encouraging to see the spirit of sacrificial volunteerism growing among elders, especially in caregiving. But where are the ones ready to exchange the comfort of an RV in a sunny location for a winter of teaching illiterates to read in their own city? Is that too much to ask?

When children never see actual acts of sacrificial caring in response to need, they have no pattern to follow. They have no spiritual capital to draw upon. They don't learn that only love is strong enough to stand up against and overcome the mystery of suffering and death. And because they don't know how to care sacrificially, deeply, they don't know their responsibility to ease the injustices of the world and restore people to the family of God. We can't live on the memory of the heroism of previous generations. We have to

The second year I was a student at a Bible college in Winnipeg, my income was about $30 to $35 a month working in the college office, hardly enough to pay my expenses. But I had saved a little from my previous job, so when the school started a building fund I donated $50 and felt good about that. The treasurer of the board who knew what I was being paid, wanted to return my check to me. He said it was too much for a student to give. He knew how little most of us students had. But I insisted I wanted to give it.

Today I wonder if I would be willing to donate more than my monthly income to some cause I believed in greatly and then trust the Lord to provide. I have lost something of the spirit of sacrifice in the years since then.

My older friend Esther Hiebert Ebel of Hillsboro, Kansas, told me about her father's spirit of sacrifice to keep Tabor College, a Mennonite Brethren school of higher learning, afloat during the 1930s. When she was about 11 or 12, she had been hoping to finally get a new pair of Sunday shoes in fall. But one evening her father came home from town to tell the family he had mortgaged the farm to help the school make needed payments. Her shoes would have to wait. Through this she learned a lesson in family sacrificial giving.

keep replenishing the capital stock in each generation with actual heroic actions.

From the Anabaptist times we have numerous stories of people who risked their lives for the cause of Christ. Mennonite history adds others, particularly Russian Mennonite history, when scores of adults surrendered their lives to prison and death to remain true to God's word. The stories of the audacity of their faith stir our inner beings.

Yet we are using up the accumulated spiritual energy of the past when we don't keep adding to the spiritual capital. We need to keep replenishing that store of spiritual energy through stories of heroes of faith today—stories that tell of courage to rise above circumstances, and persevere in spite of obstacles, stories of self-sacrifice and yielding. These are the true hero stories. These are believable heroes.

People are more likely to be inspired by imaginative writing than by creeds and statements of faith. If life has had meaning for a person, the account of that life will often have meaning for readers. A true biographer is able to separate the elements of a person's life that have meaning beyond the little community in which the person may have lived and beyond the many ordinary people who were family and friends. What was the dream, the vision, the goal in the heart that gave a life significance and urged it on? What was the secret of the life? That is what we want the young to catch a glimpse of—this vision that will strike a spark within them.

Heroes don't look like heroes. The task of the older generations is to sort through life and help the young identify the heroes. In a materialistic age, where the media pays attention to the person willing to spend more than a million dollars for a dress that actress Marilyn Monroe wore to sing "Happy Birthday" to President John Kennedy, the noble deeds of heroes have a hard time being noticed. In an age driven by the business world, greatness tends to be measured by prominence, ability, position, politics, financial assets, and personality. Yet, as an *Utne Reader* article said, celebrity-worship is a "virulent killer of fundamental human values, and the only way to control it is to quit believing in it."

Often the heroes are lost in our midst because they resemble servants in jeans and T-shirts and not glamorous celebrities in slinky gowns and tuxedos.

At the washing of the disciples' feet, Jesus said, in effect: "Be servants one of another. Do what I have done to build up the body, to bring about unity in the body, to produce maturity." Yet the power role, the celebrity role, has a way of getting to us. We flock to those who have an aura of glamour and control.

The servant-hero is the one who washes other people's feet, who enters imaginatively into the needs of others. He or she sees that it is uncomfortable to dine with

After my daughter Christine's death at age 45 in 2000, a friend wrote me the following letter. Christine had struggled with health problems for many years, but always chose to serve the underprivileged with what strength she had. For about a year and half until another health setback she worked as a clinic nurse at Venture House, a local social service agency working with the homeless and street people. You judge if she was a hero.

My friend Peg writes that she had been invited to be on the Board of Directors of Venture House, so she asked to spend a day there observing. She was allowed to sit and look on as the clients were interviewed at the reception desk. She helped serve lunch in the cafeteria. One highlight of the day was hearing about the work the nurses do.

Peg writes: "They not only take temps and refer to physicians when
(continued)

unwashed feet. It is more uncomfortable to dine without food. It is even more uncomfortable, and even painful, to live with the oppression of arrogant power. It is demeaning to be considered less than a whole person. A servant-hero has a liberating vision for other people and sees them through Christ's eyes as able to be transformed by his power and grace.

The power of a servant-hero is to move into the realm of powerlessness, setting aside patterns of authority and control, and transferring to the weak the power of decision making. This is a conscious choice. This is what the young need to see.

A rabbi was asked the difference between a true and false prophet. He answered that there was no way. If there were a way, if one had a gauge to slip over the head of the prophet and establish without question that the person was a true prophet, there would be no human dilemma and life would have no meaning.

So with the servant-hero. The servant-hero is a puzzle and a challenge. Celebrities are easily identified by the hoopla that accompanies the trappings of success, and the way people bow before them, like untouchable royalty. Servant-heroes have no such identification. They are a mystery to the world. Without fanfare they attract others to Christ. They demonstrate human possibilities and inspire young people to embark on heroic ventures.

The congregation as hero. Heroism isn't just for individuals. A congregation can also be heroic in decisions it makes with regard to its programs, emphases, and theological decisions. Some congregations stand out because they dare to risk in areas of social justice, others because they take an unpopular theological stance. I heard of one congregation that mortgaged its church plant in order to send more money to a famine-ridden country overseas. Youth should be aware of all the decisions that took the church forward in reaching outward sacrificially and the spiritual energy that the congregation invested in their formulation.

necessary, they also serve, with love, the people who suffer from simple ailments of the street—blistered feet and loneliness among them. The day I was there I sat quietly in a corner of an exam room and saw a nurse bring in an older man who was shuffling in pain. She asked him to take off his shoes and said she'd be back in a minute. She returned with a large wash pan of warm water, soap, a washcloth, and a pair of clean socks. He'd had trouble with his shoes, fumbling with his laces. She knelt at his feet, took off his shoes and socks, and slowly, carefully, washed his feet.

"I almost cried. This dirty old man and that kind nurse truly showed me, for the first time, the real meaning of the Bible story of washing feet. That day I made up my mind to accept the challenge. I served on their board of directors for I think three years
(continued)

because of what that experience taught me. So when much later I asked who was the nurse on duty, the name Wiebe did not mean anything to me until I saw her obituary in the paper [listing her as a clinic nurse at Venture House]. I appreciate and am humbled by a lesson taught to me by a nurse whom I never met." (Used by permission)

A congregation encourages heroism when it teaches and preaches a theology of calling. A hero is a person with a sense of destiny—Christian destiny. Career guidance and such matters are important, but finding one's talent is not yet finding one's gift. This sense of calling despite tremendous hurdles kept servant-heroes going.

But back to young Holden Caulfield. To grow up he had to come to terms with the imperfect adult world whether he liked it or not. And today's adults must keep showing the Holdens of this present world the imperfect heroes in their midst so that they have courage to keep reaching for the Gold Ring.

Now try this:

1. Have a "This Is Your Life" evening, in which young and old together present the life of one of the older members of the congregation who has served faithfully and sacrificially.

2. Have someone in the congregation include a short biography of an elder in each church newsletter. Focus not on what the person achieved and how many countries he or she traveled to, but on the journey of the inner terrain of the soul. What spiritual hurdles did this man or woman conquer by the grace of God?

3. Have the young people list their heroes. Have the elders do the same. Do the lists overlap?
4. Do we encourage pride when we publicize and honor heroic lives?

Chapter 10

If Only People Ask

Elders have no wisdom unless they are asked to share it.
Unless someone draws it out of them, it remains as hidden
as the gold in an undiscovered mine.

"When you get older," Sadie Delany said, "you ask yourself, 'How have I run my life? Did I live it well?' . . . When you live a long time, you have stories to tell. If only people [would] ask."

Yes, if only people would ask. Amy Hill Hearth asked. She helped the African-American sisters Sadie and Bessie Delany write their life story. The result was the best seller *Having Our Say*. Bessie died at age 104 in 1996. Sadie died in 1999 at age 109 in the Mount Vernon, New York, home the sisters shared.

I hear often that older generations are willing to pass on their wisdom by telling their experiences, but the younger generations aren't interested. They don't ask. What Grandpa or Grandma did when they were in high school isn't as important or exciting as what the high schoolers are going to be doing tonight at the basketball game and after it. It doesn't help to force a story on them.

"Just as a falling tree makes a noise when someone hears, so a person's life lessons really exist when someone else thinks the lessons are important enough to learn and meaningful enough to remember," writes Helen Q. Kivnick in *Remembering and Being Remembered*. Bluntly stated, elders have no wisdom unless they are asked to share it. Unless someone draws it out of them, it remains as hidden as the gold in an undiscovered lode.

Not all children and grandchildren can inherit the same candlestick or Fostoria dinnerware, but the same "jewel of wisdom" can enrich a whole generation of grandchildren—if they ask for it.

One task to connect the generations is to convince the young that a grandparent's jewel of wisdom is worth more than the candlestick or dishes. It's the last chance grandchildren will have to understand their family histories and where they fit into that history. It's the last chance to clear up mysteries and misstatements about family members and their marriages, deaths, decisions, and journeyings. It's their last chance to learn where the source of strength and resilience resided in previous generations.

Richard E. Wentz relates a Jewish woman's story about a time during World War II when four elderly Jews in a tiny Polish village were carried off in the back of a truck. One of them, a musician, was holding an expensive cello. The occupants were destined for the concentration camp.

A young German lieutenant crawled into the van and clambered across legs and ammunition to stop in front of the old musician and his cello. "You will not need that, where you are going. We have no room for it here, no time for it!" He threw the cello onto the street where it smashed to bits on the stones.

Wentz reports his reaction to the old woman's story was that "nothing accompanies you to annihilation." Her response to him was that the image of the broken cello was left! "Keep that memory; that's what's left."

I think of elders who came to this land with very little in terms of artifacts. They had only their language,

My elderly Aunt Neta living in Moscow with a daughter and her family told me a story in 1989 I will never forget. Her older sister Tina and family living in the Ukraine had been exiled to the north in the early 1930s under Stalin's regime. After World War II Aunt Neta, a widow with four young children, was transported by cattle car to the Kazakhstan area to do hard labor in the forest and construction industry. Life was extremely difficult for her. But after Stalin's death in 1953, the detainees in this area were more free to travel. Aunt Neta made it her mission to visit all her sisters in Siberia, including Aunt Tina, far away in the Perm area.

She had a destination and an address. In 1956 she wrote her sister Tina when she would be starting her journey but not when she would arrive. Travel was too indefinite at the time. At her arrival in the large city she

(continued)

memories, hopes, and dreams. These don't need money to survive. But they need an audience. Even those who were born and raised in this country have a story to tell. All elders need an audience.

When the young talk to their elders, this is the younger generation's chance to pass on their experiences, albeit only a decade or more old. Their insights into life, even from a short perspective of ten to 15 years, encourages and revives an older person and shows them again what childlikeness is. Reciprocal generativity—all generations teaching one another—is not a clear concept in a society strongly tuned to the idea that only the elders have a story to tell or something to teach.

Not everyone moving into the older years will be able to write his or her life wisdom into a book. But the sharing of stories with younger generations, including the boomers, must not be neglected.

Why tell your life experiences?

Stories provide patterns of living. On the fourth day of creation God created the lights, giving us night and day and winter and summer. Was this just an impulse on God's part? Hardly. God had a plan in mind. Yet when God imagined and created night and day, God had no pattern to follow. No one had prepared a pattern like I use when I knit a sweater or that carpenters follow when they build a house.

When God created the sun and the moon, God had no astronomic models on the lab table to follow. When God made a tree, there was no encyclopedia to explain what it looked like. When God made a spider, there wasn't a science textbook to indicate how many legs it had. Unlike us mortals, who need models when we make something,

pondered where to go to find her sister, and started walking.

Across the street she saw a woman whose demeanor and walk resembled the sister she had seen last 25 years ago at their father's funeral in the Ukraine. She called out, "Tina!" No response. She called again, "Tina!" The woman turned and recognized her sister. They hugged and cried. "When you called out Tina," said the older woman, "I never recognized my own name. My children call me Mama, and since my husband's death, no one has called me by my first name."

I cherish this story and the many others she told me. My Aunt Neta had a need to tell it. How often will she have rehearsed this story of God's providence in her mind and hoped some day to tell it to the extended family?

In James Michener's novel The Covenant *the old grandmother is dying. The would-be preacher recognizes the dying grandmother possesses words of importance that ought to be passed from one generation to the next. So he assembles the entire family in the sick-room and declares to them: "This Ouma who lies here with us has had a powerful life, and you must know about it, and tell it to your children's children."*

And so the elderly Wilhelmina tells the story of how she came to DeKraal in South Africa. Through her story she affirms to children and grandchildren who they are and invites them to reflect upon their own experience. She is saying, "We belong together. We're family. This is a pattern you must hold onto."

God created entirely out of his imagination. God didn't have to worry whether it looked like the real thing. There was no real thing. The real thing was in God's mind.

But you and I need patterns, or blueprints, to build a house, to fashion a garment—even to build character. Before you build a human life after God's pattern, you need to know what that pattern looks like.

Stories are basically patterns. Faith got started in storytelling. After the resurrection, Jesus gave Mary the command to "tell the disciples the story of what you have seen." Those who came later asked the original witnesses to tell them the stories of Jesus, and his presence was renewed.

In what are known as the storytelling psalms, the psalmist tells the Israelites stories of how God had dealt with them as a people and which they were to use to keep going. Psalm 78 is one such psalm probably recited at a festival of the Israelite people.

"We will tell the next generation the praiseworthy deeds

of the Lord, his power, and the wonders he has done," the psalmist writes (v. 4). "So the next generation would know them, even the children yet to be born, and they in turn would tell their children. Then they would put their trust in God and would not forget his deeds but would keep his commands" (vv. 6-7).

Stories are powerful hero-makers as the poems and songs of the Middle Ages testify. Beowulf's prowess lived on because people kept his story alive.

Elder tales pass on a shared and collective identity. In a very mobile society, storytelling gives children greater stability and security if they know where they came from. It gives them a sense of identity, of place, of values: "This is where I belong."

Sociologists tell us that one out of two or three families moves every year. Some families have lost all contact with their past. Their root system has dried up.

Instead of finding a sense of identity in their family's values, they are forced to relate to the many places the family has lived and possibly the television shows and movies they saw in each place—*Sesame Street* in Alberta, *Wizard of Oz* in California, *Gone with the Wind* in Kansas. Both younger and older people are asking, "Who am I? Where did I come from?" This interest is apparent in the widespread genealogy searches being conducted by all ages.

Answers may not be available because Grandpa and Grandma live on the West Coast and the children are somewhere far removed. Therefore, they don't see each other often. It may also be that there are so many grandparents because of merged families, it is hard for a child to keep all the relatives sorted out.

A person without a sense of "personal history" is a detached person, like an engine loose in a housing, unable to connect, and ready to break family ties if need

My husband died shortly after we had moved to Kansas in fall 1962, leaving me with four young children far away from family and familiar surroundings. I often felt very discouraged. For a long time I kept a little note from my father in distant Saskatchewan tacked to my bulletin board: "Don't forget you are a Funk."

I don't know exactly what he meant by those words, but to me they meant he expected me to keep going as he and his family had stood steady when the ground shook with agony and despair during the Russian Revolution and then later in Canada during the Depression. I recalled some of the stories he had told me of his childhood as his parents had told him stories of their early lives. He was bequeathing to me whatever family strengths there were for such situations. His few words gave me hope.

Family strength is not
(continued)

be to succeed in life. Likewise, a person without a strong sense of congregational or denominational history is most ready to pick up and go elsewhere when the going gets rough or dissatisfying.

The Israelites reaffirmed again and again, "I am an Israelite of the tribe of Abraham, Isaac, and Jacob. We are God's people. We belong to God. At times we didn't want to follow him and were disobedient. But God received us again and again."

Elder tales versus preacher stories. Preachers use stories to serve their theological propositions. They become illustrations, an add-on, something that can be cut if the sermon is too long. Yet if the story is energy-laden and integral to the sermon, it overtakes the sermon because it is a living thing and cannot be held back or deleted for the sake of time.

A real story is about emotional relationships, ours to God, God to ours, ours to other people. Facts, propositions, can be passed on by impersonal memo, but only feelings, convictions, and beliefs come through in personal sharing of stories.

When stories are distilled and packaged for popular consumption into dull theological systems, they do not capture the imagination of the listener. One writer said that we must recover the story if we are to recover a faith for our day. Each of us has a story. Alongside it is the Christian faith story. The way the two stories interweave and affect one another can have a profound influence on the listener, deep enough to cause him or her to say, "That's my story too," or "I want that to be my story too."

Stories make it possible to transcend the moment and reach into another realm, that of mystery, emotions, and even ambiguity. Today television, movies, and musicians have become our storytellers, but they don't bond themselves to the audience, which is the true task of the elder storyteller.

Imagine the Mennonite community without the stories of the Anabaptist martyrs, without Peter J. Dyck's won-

accidental. It needs to be nurtured and primed. For many years our family priming came from a small family newsletter published by my brother Jack until ill health forced him to stop. As Jack himself admitted, he never let mere facts get in the way of the truth of a story. Like a gopher, he dug for truth. Sometimes his facts got stretched beyond belief to fit his case, and then when we got together we spent hours arguing facts, never truth.

In a sense my brother is right. What difference does it make whether something happened in 1943 or 1945? Or whether the house was two blocks from school or three? Hanging onto the truth of the story was important. That truth bound us together.

derful accounts of how God helped the Mennonite refugees after World War II, without C. F. Klassen's words *"Gott kann"* (God can). The way God brought hope to hundreds of refugees whose lives had been ravaged by war and revolution, famine and disease inspired those who heard their story.

Stories tell a child what difference faith makes in a person's life. Young people have difficulty seeing how God is at work in their family, the congregation, or society as a whole. Sometimes it is even difficult for elders when health fails, children move away, and expenses rise. When I taught a college class in the Psalms, I had the students write their own lament psalm, following the structural pattern of the psalmist. One section of the lament looks into the past recalling the times when God worked in the psalmist's life.

In their own psalms, this "looking-back" section was often the most difficult part, even when the students came from strong Christian backgrounds. It was easy for them to see what money can do for the family. It buys houses, a second or third vehicle, CDs, computers, vacations, fad clothing. But where was the evidence of the working of God? They couldn't see it because of the lack of awareness and because they hadn't lived long enough to know it when they saw it. Too few people had ever pointed out to them God's hand in daily lives in learning to forgive, to love, to be faithful.

If I asked you to tell me about your God, you might answer with a confessional statement. God is loving, kind, and forgiving. God is all-powerful, all-knowing, all-caring. God expects us to live and serve him.

When you tell me your story, you tell me about the God you actually worship. Your true faith is revealed in your story. The psalmist told stories about passing through the Red Sea as if on dry land, about being fed with manna, about God giving the Israelites quails to eat. He doesn't omit their rebellion against God when they forgot God's sustaining power at the entrance to the Promised Land.

For the psalmist, however, history was not just something that happened back there. He was conscious that God worked in the lives of the Israelites in the past and that God continued to work. The Israelites' story continued to the present.

Stories promote intergenerational understanding. Stories give listeners room to work on what the story means to them. They challenge old and young to examine the story at their own level of experience and understanding. A teenager may examine the rich young ruler's sincere attempt to find the way to eternal life and ponder his or her own attachment to fad clothes and cars. A woman of 80 may understand better how clinging to her small heap of possessions has kept her from true riches over the years.

Stories keep oral history alive. One way children can find their place in the continuity of the family's experience is by hearing oral tales of bygone events. This feeling of continuity was once taken for granted, especially in ethnic groups, when families lived close together. Some of these oral tales may have achieved the status of legend and folktale, but they are important nonetheless. They illuminate certain periods in a family's history, often a turning point or crisis.

I suggested to a Native American who I knew had many stories to tell that he write down his many experiences of his tribe. He objected strenuously. He wanted no part of writing, only of telling and telling and

My parents told us children a story of how my father risked his life shortly after the Russian revolution to travel by foot a long distance from home to the place where Mother's parents were last known to have lived. She had lost track of them during the revolution and anarchy that followed.

I worked at piecing the story together over a period of years, but hesitated to tell it or write it down for fear my audience wouldn't understand how precious the story was to me. It wasn't just another adventure story about someone who was crazy enough to travel into the fearsome unknown to find his new wife's relatives.

Then on one occasion, at a writer's conference, I risked telling the story. I put my arms around them with this story. As I spoke, suddenly I sensed a strange silence come over the audience and saw someone wipe a tear. That was
(continued)

retelling his children and grandchildren the story of his tribe's history. Oral tales that indicated Sally Hemings, the slave mistress of Thomas Jefferson, had mothered numerous children by him, were passed down from generation to generation. Recently they were reinforced by DNA testing of those who had told themselves for generations they were descendants of this union. Yet their oral history alone ·kept their convictions alive.

In her family history *The Merging*, Evelyn King Mumaw tells the story of the Swiss William Tell who was goaded into showing off his supreme marksmanship by shooting an apple off his son's head with his bow and arrow. Most children know the outcome of this event. Yet the story takes on special significance because Evelyn, a seventh generation King, was told by her sixth generation father Irvin King that some elderly relatives had told him that some of their ancestors had been present that day in Altdorfer Village when William Tell shot the arrow from his son's head. This bit of oral history gave validity to the Swiss Anabaptist roots of the Koenig (King) family.

Here's a little oral story out of my own roots. My mother told me that as a young girl in the Ukraine she spent one summer with her widowed grandmother in Molotschna. As they sat outside in the evening air a man rode up and asked for her grandmother. He handed her a parcel and rode off. She and her grandmother opened it to find a beautiful family photo. Her grandmother passed it off as some relative's picture and placed it in a drawer. That night she watched her grandmother sit alone in a dark room and cry. From time to time my mother sneaked a look at the picture in the drawer.

That same winter her grandmother became sick and Mother had to write her children to come. When the children arrived, my mother was eager to show them the beautiful picture, for such a professional photograph was a rarity. When she went to the bureau drawer to find it, it was gone. Her elderly sick grandmother acted as if she didn't know what the child was talking about.

But the story began to unravel at her deathbed. In her youth she had worked in a saloon in Prussia and had given birth to several children without telling anyone. The picture was probably of her children in their adoptive home. The story has no great moral lesson for me other than to reinforce how human my forebears were. And that somewhere, somewhere, in Russia, there is a branch of my family I will never know about.

the first time I sensed the true power of story-telling. I risked in telling the story, but I remained true to my story, and the story was launched. It was later published as a chapter in The Storekeeper's Daughter *by Herald Press.*

Stories benefit the elders. Stories are hugs, embraces. A storyteller, whether a child of five sharing a kindergarten experience or an elder telling the story of picking berries, reaches out with words to draw the listener close. He or she tells the listener or reader, "I trust you with the specialness of my story. It belongs to me but now I give it to you." Good storytellers soon learn that the more personal their story, the more universal it is.

When someone truly listens, that person is present to the storyteller, and transmits to the teller the same feeling as when someone responds to a genuine embrace. When the young generation takes time to listen to an older person reminisce, they affirm to that person: "Who you are and what you have experienced is important to me. You are giving me the gift of your life and wisdom." Stories teach trust in interdependence and give the elders emotional reinforcement.

Sharing their life story helps the older generation to retrieve spiritual resources within themselves, to harvest the past like a farmer harvests a field, and to hand it over to the young of all ages. Recalling a time when they felt as if they had the world by the tail, when hurdles fell before them, when they dealt adequately with losses, can again give the elders a sense of control and stability.

Yet the biggest obstacle to generations sharing their stories is the logistics one. When and where can this storytelling take place in a society in which each age-group is busy, too busy to listen to Grandma Yoder talk about what happened when she was a young girl in a snowstorm at school?

What forum works for elders to present their stories?

We often think first of a public setting. Very possibly, the best time is not in formal "reminiscing" sessions, nor in Bible classes, in eulogies at funerals, in retreats, extended family dinners, or church celebrations, although all these settings should make room for story-telling. Among older generations the reminiscing can become more formal. Teens typically don't like to be col-lared and told they are now expected to sit and listen. They don't like eye-to-eye contact like young children do. Stories will have to slide into their lives obliquely.

In our day, it is important to prepare a new vehicle for one generation to share its wisdom with another. That new way may be the old way while engaged in the tradi-tional roles of parent and child—around the table while eating, while cooking or filling the dishwasher, while learning a new skill, while communicating through e-mail, while driving to and from softball practice, while getting ready for bed. I have lots of stories to tell. With my grandchildren I try to do it through e-mail. With my adult children the best time is over a cup of tea at the kitchen table, the way my mother and dad told me their stories. But that means I have to have stories ready to tell.

A number of years ago for our church's centennial observation I wrote a short story about some famous character in the congregation's history as an insert in the weekly worship folder. I hoped people, young and old, in a captive situation, perhaps bored, would read the story and remember it.

Children and adults are both reading the Harry Potter tales these days as I work on this manuscript, mainly because both age-groups enjoy the same emotional con-tent. An authentic story relates to all ages and all stages of faith development.

I'd like to see more older adults share their struggle in a search for personal meaning. I sense that now that I am over 70, I am still looking at people older than I am to find out what life will be like when lived with Christ's

A friend told a story at a gathering of elders of her farm family's experience in western Kansas during the dust bowl years. Daily life meant coping with dust and more dust. Faye's telling came alive when she shared the desperation of her parents when their only cow died and her infant sister needed milk. Her father walked a considerable distance every day to a neighbor to get a small pail of milk. One time he got lost in the dense clouds of dust that darkened the day. The mother in desperation and against her better judgment sent the 13-year-old son into the darkness of the dust storm to find his father with firm instructions to go no further than his small flashlight could guide him.

At long last son and father stumbled into the house, the father completely exhausted, face crusted with dirt, gasping for breath, but still clutching the precious little pail of milk. One
(continued)

daily presence at age 80. Is there still joy? Is there still hope? What gives meaning at that time in life?

Here's a story I don't want to forget about life at 90: After one of my annual visits to see my mother in Edmonton, I turned to her to say good-bye. Mother made her usual comment that this might be the last time we would see each other. But her next words will never leave me. She was in her nineties, living alone, often lonely because of her inability to move around easily. Most of her friends had died. Yet she told me though she was ready for death, she preferred to live "because life is still so sweet." She gave me hope in growing old.

I liked what the Lorraine Avenue Mennonite Church in Wichita did during a pastoral transition. Someone had attached a lengthy time chart of the church's story to a wall. The chart was at least 20 to 30 feet long with major time divisions in the church's history clearly marked, but thereafter anyone could add details. And they did. All sorts of little details had been added at appropriate dates about the lives of members as well as the life of the congregation. As I studied it, I sensed the church members were pointing out the Exodus, the times when manna fell from heaven, when they drank water from a rock, when God fought the battle, in their own story.

listener commented: "This should be called a story of courage." Unfortunately the large audience included no one under the age of 65 or 70.

As I mentioned earlier, Psalm 137 tells a little story full of emotion about life as an alien in a foreign land. In Babylon the Hebrews longed for their homeland. In honest, almost brutal language, the writer expresses a desperate yearning for the land left behind and the anger at having been torn away. This psalm is not often read in public, especially the last verses, because of its violent feelings, yet these high-pitched emotions give it power and authenticity.

Emotions haven't changed since the creation of humanity. They remain the same: what the prodigal feels like when coming home to warmth and love instead of to rejection, the stark fear of facing the person one has wronged (Jacob facing Esau), the horror of violence and war (Deborah's prayer), despair when the bank account is empty (the widow of Zarephath), the pain of dissension in the home (Eli and his sons), the experience of God's mercy and grace (David's forgiveness).

Hope is always hope, love is always love, courage is always courage. Faith in Christ is always faith in Christ whether it is the desperate little Zacchaeus trying to see Jesus or a despairing young adult longing for a chance to try again.

As the listener identifies with the emotion in the story, he or she finds God's pattern for holy living. The

Hebrews told and retold their story of God's redemption at every public gathering. "We were oppressed, but God delivered us. We grumbled, but God forgave. We were in need, God provided. God's faithful love never left us."

These are the kinds of stories the younger generation needs to hear so that they can say with the Israelites, "As you took care of the Israelites, as you took care of my parents, you will take care of me." This is the pattern we want to follow.

A deer's footprints in the snow in my backyard remained a long time after the rest of the snow had melted. So do ours when we tell stories. It is important to talk about our stories, our encounters with the holy, with others, for out of this kind of sharing of stories comes a common faith.

Now try this:

1. What is your story of personal redemption? Have you told your children and grandchildren this story? Why not? As members of the historic peace churches we should have countless stories of forgiveness and personal reconciliation in our history, yet these are hard to find. Why has practical forgiveness been neglected in favor of position papers about peace?

2. What story of God's sufficient help in time of trial do you have? Have you told your children and grandchildren this story? What story in your life do you hesitate to share with others? Why?

3. God's power and leading is often more identifiable by looking back than by making assertions about the immediate situation. Do you agree?

4. Church life often becomes heavy with theological assumptions and propositions overlaid with a thin icing of good feelings. The Christian life should be the breeding ground of stories of inner struggles to

reach higher ground, and of personal and collective experiences in the congregation. Why is it difficult to be authentic and vulnerable in our sharing groups? Everyone has a few stories he or she is ready to share without hesitation. The deeper story is more difficult to share. What can a congregation do to make it possible to hear more faith stories that reveal true faith, not just mimicked faith?

5. What do you say to someone who remarks, "The past is the past. It's the present that's important"? Is there danger of dwelling too much in the past? Or taking the nostalgia trip too often and not getting on with life today, especially if you are older?

6. Elton Trueblood, Quaker writer, states that we desperately need a literature of witness in which persons "who have reached a firm place to stand are able to tell us the road by which they have come and why it was taken." Does your congregation have room for such people to tell their story?

7. Jewish storytelling often took place at festivals. How could we incorporate more stories and fewer sermons into church celebrations?

8. When you are homeless, in exile, a refugee, the historical account stops. Historians leave a blank because no important committee meetings were held or official decisions recorded. Yet in the midst of upheaval, even such as the Israelites experienced, the family story continues. Were you ever "homeless" or in "exile," self-imposed or otherwise? Did your story stop at that point? Or did it begin then?

10. Make a chart of the history of your church. Collect life stories of older adults. Identify changes that have taken place.

11. Keep track of what happened during the day or during the week to share with someone.

Chapter 11

Visible Reminders of Invisible Truths

*We need constant visible reminders that say to young
and old: "Feed on me. Let my Spirit sustain you.
I am the living bread."*

Can a renewed emphasis on symbols bring the generations together? The world of symbols is not something the Mennonite community has officially espoused in its history. They resemble icons and idols too closely to find a comfortable home in churches that developed out of the Anabaptist wing of the Reformation. But hear me out.

Robert Wuthnow in *Growing Up Religious* states that the two hundred adults from a variety of ethnic, religious, and economic backgrounds he interviewed for his study did not remember the doctrinal instruction they received as youths. Yet they learned a great deal. They did remember "the flannelgraph and sword drills, and the two-day little-sleep, soft-drinks-and-sleeping-bags retreat that the youth group took. What they recalled fondly about religion—and what often drew the adults back to the church—were the rituals and sacred objects that were at the center of their religious upbringings."

Lauren F. Winner, in her article "Sword Drills and Stained Glass in *Christianity Today*, agrees that "the incense and crosses and leisurely lunches after church rather than the intricacies of the doctrine of atonement" have an impact on children. In other words, the emotional impact of the symbols and rituals of the faith stayed with them, not always the words.

What is a symbol?

Symbols are tremendously powerful to bring about change. A symbol bridges two realities—the real and concrete, the abstract and intangible. It is something that stands for something else. A lion is often thought of as a symbol of courage, so when the cowardly lion in *The Wizard of Oz* lacks courage, the audience identifies with him. They know what it means to be scared.

When we move into the realm of symbols, we move into a world where we keep crossing these two realities of the real and the abstract. The appearance of a rainbow after a rain reminds us that God promised not to destroy the natural order. It is a visual reminder of the grace and mercy of the Creator.

A common symbol is the flag, a piece of cloth with a design on it. In itself a flag is weak and powerless, yet it takes on enormous strength, greater than the mightiest weapon of war, when recognized as the symbol of a nation. A flag has been known to inspire unbelievable energy and daring by soldiers in time of war. The flag bearer carried it at the head of the army to keep the men strong.

When the meaning of a symbol is grasped, it has greater power to exert good in the world than armies, rifles, and bombs have to perform evil. Symbols can sweep people into new areas of thought with their power as the peace symbol did during the 1960s. A symbol like the lily of the field is an invitation to become still and wonder and to reach into a realm beyond the prosaic dullness of human experience, for lilies "toil not, neither do they spin."

During the 1960s African-Americans discovered symbolic power and effected sweeping social change by introducing new symbols. Suddenly African names that were hard to pronounce and harder to spell gave us pause. We saw bushy Afros and the black fist lifted in challenge. We heard rap music. Thousands of blacks found themselves caught up in the power of these new life-giving symbols. Freedom was on its way. When particularly new strong symbols emerge, for a while society is forced to decide whether to accept or reject this new meaning drifting in and out of consciousness. Some people never make a choice and flounder.

Worship music A good example of change being influenced by the force of changing symbols is the new direction worship music is taking congregations. A hymn, a praise song, or a chorus is always more than just a group of words set to music. For any worshiper a specific hymn or chorus can become a symbol of a spiritual experience. Choruses and hymns chart the inner journey of believers. They formulate their theology of faith.

When I was a child I learned "The B-I-B-L-E, yes, that's the book for me." That song still evokes memories of vacation Bible school, sword drills, and flannel graph lessons and a simple childlike faith. As a young adult I sang choruses such as "For God So Loved the World." To sing "Dare to Be a Daniel" inspired me with courage. Later on, hymns became more important. "How Great Thou Art" still speaks hope and courage to me; others bring comfort, and still others remind me of faith decisions I made at various points in my journey. Each song is both a song and a symbol.

When elders come to church Sunday after Sunday to hear only new praise choruses, sometimes with a disturbing beat that hurts their eardrums, they feel disoriented. They have lost powerful symbols of their faith that regularly drew them into the presence of God. Those hymns reminded them of the familiar Lord to whom they had committed themselves. Who is this strange new God who invites to noise and discomposure? For the young, a worship team with brass and drums and a lively beat tells them in very certain terms, "This church knows where it's at! That's the kind of God I want to worship."

Old Testament symbols

Old Testament Hebrews had many symbols given them by God to keep reminding them who they belonged to. The words God spoke through the prophets and priests weren't enough. These symbols included the various feasts the Hebrews celebrated and places they considered holy, like the temple and Bethel, where Jacob met God. The pillars of fire and cloud that accompanied the children of Israel through the wilderness denoted the Lord's presence. The Sabbath and circumcision identified them as being in covenant with God. Names and numbers in the Old Testament often carried symbolic truth. Here are a few other symbols we don't usually think about.

Standing stones were common symbols representing a reality—an object, event, and value associated with the stone. Some of you may have spent time picking stones from a field and wished you'd never see another one. What is a stone? Something very inert, dumb, lifeless. Something at the lower end of our scale of importance. A stone is the image of deadness, yet the concordance has about 270 references to stones in the Bible, many with symbolic life-giving meaning.

On four occasions Jacob erected a *massebah* (a standing stone) after a significant event in his life: Once after his dream in which God spoke to him from the top of a stairway reaching to heaven (Gen. 28:10-22); again after he left the pagan world of Laban, his father-in-law (Gen. 31:45-54); third, at Bethel, where he wrestled with the angel of the Lord (Gen. 35:14-15). The last time was at his wife Rachel's grave near Bethlehem (Gen. 35:20), as a reminder of his beloved wife.

But there were other occasions when *massebahs* were raised. Seven times Joshua erected standing stones pointing to the power of God. The first time was after the people crossed the Jordan. A person from each tribe brought a stone to erect a memorial in the middle of the shallow riverbed. Later on, when the people saw the stones and asked, "What do these stones mean?" the leaders were to answer, "Israel crossed the Jordan on dry ground."

Any time we are finished with one aspect of our lives, when we have crossed a Jordan, it is important to find something visible with which to build a memorial so that young and old passing by will ask, "What does this mean?" And the answer always is the working of God's grace in our lives.

Manna jar. God knew the Israelites were a forgetful people. So God had their priests tie a piece of string around their collective finger. They were to take a measure of manna and put it in a golden jar to be lodged in the ark of the covenant together with Aaron's budding rod. There it would be preserved for the generations to come "so they can see the bread I gave you to eat in the desert when I brought you out of Egypt." The manna jar was to be a visible reminder to young and old of God's help at a crucial point in their lives (Exod. 16:31-34).

What the Israelites were likely to forget

Slavery in Egypt. They were likely to forget where they had come from—that they had been slaves in bondage to the Egyptians for 400 years. They were likely to forget the pain of the overseers' lashes.

The Exodus. They were likely to forget the Exodus, that great event when God opened the waters of the Red Sea and brought them to the other side on dry land. God saved them. They hadn't escaped on their own. God knew that successive generations of Israelites might be tempted to think they had always lived in the Promised Land, that the Egyptian interlude of slavery never happened. The manna jar was to remind them they had a different history.

God's daily care. They were likely to forget that God had taken care of their needs day by day in the wilderness. Each of the 600,000 men plus women and children needed food. Their stomachs growled with hunger. In the desert they grumbled. Egypt's leeks and garlic looked great compared to their present fare. Were they going to die here?

Then God fed them manna and quail. Thin white flakes like frost appeared on the ground. It tasted like honey. We think of any wilderness experience as a place of deprivation—tough, demanding. For the Israelites it was a place of sufficiency, of enoughness, and of economic equality because God provided for all. No one ever lacked enough food to eat. God took care of them. But they were likely to forget God's daily provision when they settled into their own food-production in Canaan.

A people of God. They were likely to forget that they were to be a people of God, a body in covenant relationship with God, not just a group of individuals who had begun a journey together. Binding them together was God's faithful, abiding love. At the beginning of their trek they weren't a bonded people, other than having a common ancestry. But the desert experience brought them together into a body, a people.

The message of the manna jar was "Let this be a reminder to you that I am the one who delivered you."

Jacques Ellul in *Living Faith* writes that our civilization is a people without a memory. We forget very soon what happened just a few years ago or even a decade ago. Collectively we forget events like wars, persecutions, wanderings in the desert, "all things that past generations in their obstinate will to live managed to overcome." Ellul's point is that memory should inoculate us against knowingly entering the same kind of experience again. It should remind us how to act in the future.

"People in our society are creatures without memory; step by step they forget everything. This means that they have no past and no roots. And so these people have no foreseeable future and no past to build on," writes Ellul.

Today we are people without a manna jar or standing stones in congregational life. We have too few visible reminders of what has happened in the faith pilgrimage of our family and our church outside our historical centers. If we forget the past we lack roots, we have nothing to hold us firmly when life becomes difficult. People without a memory are the fearful, the violent, the rigid. We need visible, concrete items to remind us that as God was with us in the past, God will continue with us in the future. We need symbols that children see often and are explained to them.

What we are likely to forget

Our own exodus. Our own exodus from a life without Christ to a life with Christ. Our salvation experience may have happened so long ago or been such a little rip-ple in our life journey as a child that it doesn't seem like a significant experience any more when compared to that of modern movie action pictures. Faith stories told to the congregation aren't as common as when I was a child.

Our wilderness wanderings. The memory of our wilderness experiences and how God walked with us during that period—and that there was enough—is often tossed aside during good times. Good health, good jobs, well-behaved children, peace in the land, the choice of dozens of modes of communicating with one anoth-er—have ways of making us neglect to tell our children of God's provision in our wilderness wandering.

We are a people of God. In an era of self-reliance and independent living, we may forget that we are a people, the body of Christ, not just a group of happy individuals who pump hands vigorously and smile generously at one another during greeting time on Sunday morning. We are covenanted to God and to one another to bring glory to our Creator and Lord. All believers, young and old, belong to this body.

Can you be a Christian without the church? More and more I have my doubts. Children and youth learn early that to belong to a church is a bother, for it means devel-oping relationships, accountability, and service—and lis-tening to dull or superficial sermons at times. Church has become a Sunday morning affair, with little or no contact with the body throughout the week. Personal needs overwhelm. Some people hunger for greater fel-lowship but have no way of finding it in the face of widespread self-sufficiency.

Young people going to school soon become caught in

the work cycle. Even for them work to earn money for their specific needs determines the rhythms of life. Monday is now the first day of the week followed by four days of work. Saturday begins the weekend and Sunday is the second day of reprieve from work. The Lord's day followed by six days of work is no longer the norm, even in calendars. Some people admit they feel more needed at work than in the church.

Do you need anyone? Does anyone need you? The important lesson of the manna jar is that the church is a covenant body, joined to one another and to God through Christ. All believers, young and old, belong to this body. They are joined in a long march together, not as individuals, but as a body in bringing about the kingdom of God. Yet as the generations become fragmented and more individualistic, this sense of unity is slowly lost.

Today's goal is individual personal security before God. Religion today is a religion of the private sphere for many people, not an intergenerational whole. Faith gives daily strength, a sense of meaning and direction to the individual believer, young or old. It has no great impact outside the self. Eugene Peterson in *Christ Plays in Community* adds that self-spirituality has become the hallmark of our age—a spirituality of Me—of self-centering, self-sufficiency, and self-development. Such a spirit pulls the generations apart.

Modern symbols

When the immigrants of all nationalities and religious traditions came to America, they immediately built churches, even if very humble ones, to anchor their faith. The church became the repository of the sacred symbols of the community. A woodworker built a pulpit, or "sacred desk," that was firmly planted in the center of the platform to indicate the Word of God was central to this body of believers. On it was placed the pulpit Bible.

Soon someone fashioned a communion table, and a pitcher and goblet were added to the group of sacred symbols. Pews were installed as well as hymnbooks. Church records were begun. Grave markers in the graveyard symbolized faith in eternal life. Not all these symbols have survived, at least not in the same forms. It is unfortunate that cemeteries, now called memorial gardens, are now often far removed from the church. Some children may never have walked through one and examined the inscriptions of faith on stone after stone.

Modern cultural symbols pull young and old to them—McDonald's and Pepsi, Intel and Microsoft, Nike and Tommy Hilfiger. The rich symbols of Scripture through which people understand their relationship with God have a hard time keeping up if people only encounter them once a week instead of hundreds of times like these others. Few Christian events make the headlines unless it involves a conflict. Peace, love for one another, the suffering of the cross, are not headline words nor are symbols like the dove and the cross, considered powerful ones, simply because they don't attract commercial ventures.

To make the life of faith sound more attractive, some people attempt to describe it in terms of the competitive world of sports and business—winning and losing. I sense a yearning among some Christians for new words and symbols.

We need symbols that draw us, young and old, away from the world of competitiveness and self-seeking and toward Christ.

Jesus introduced symbols for his followers to cling to. But some of these traditional Christian symbols have lost their power, partly because they are unfamiliar to today's children. Salt, packaged in those neat little throwaway tubes for fast-food establishments, doesn't convey the idea of spiritual influence.

The cross is mostly an ornament dangling on a chain, sometimes from earlobes, in what Eugene Peterson calls "boutique spirituality," or God as decoration.

Children growing up in high rise apartments have never seen a shepherd guarding his sheep grazing by still waters. The dove, which we cling to as a symbol of peace and of the Holy Spirit, is confused with the bothersome pigeons that nest in the crannies of high buildings. Lamps and candles, often referred to in Scripture, are used today mostly for the romantic touch—to cast an aura of tenderness rather than to dispel darkness.

Though we use a lot of servanthood language in the church, most children have never seen an actual servant nor do they know what the posture of servants was during Bible times. Many of them have never seen a basin and towel used together. They know that when your feet are dirty, you crawl into the shower or tub and do what is necessary there—without the help of the host.

On the other hand, children soon learn the language of competition, incivility, and violence from television, movies, and sports. Our language forces us to conceive of life as an endless win/lose struggle. Success in even the mildest endeavors is depicted in outright battlefield terminology: we grapple with, strive, lock horns, tussle, contend, engage, or take the offensive to achieve a triumph, a victory, a conquest, a win, a put down, a mastery, or a killing.

Minorities have long been aware of George Orwell's words that "if thought corrupts language, language can also corrupt thought." They insist that words like "nigger" and "colored" be removed from linguistic currency because their use reinforces racial prejudice. I see the trend to describe the Christian life in the contemporary idiom of the competitive secular world something we need to be more wary of, for it will eventually influence our and especially our children's attitude toward life and behavior.

The language of faith (trust, hope, forgive, love, encourage, feed, aid, offer, support, sacrifice) may not make as interesting headlines as the language of competition and war (oppose, limit, denounce, defend, beat, stomp), but it is the only one which brings life to both listener and hearer.

We cannot live by bread alone. We live in strenuous times, culturally, spiritually, and economically. Something has broken—the center has not held. Things fall apart. Violent shootings repeatedly burst into the news. Revolutionary war disturbs many countries. Sexual excesses and foul language have taken over television programming.

We have developed in our society the idea that we can live by what is offered by advertisers alone. Children are being brought up to believe that a certain measure of wealth is their right—a telephone, a stereo, a car when they are old enough to drive, money for ski equipment, and eating out. Families demand certain rights—a vacation away from home each year, a television in every room, a separate bathroom for each person in which every towel and tile matches. Older adults demand the right to travel often each year and find new experiences to keep their lives from signaling emptiness.

Yet people in their spiritual hunger come to Jesus like the crowd did in John 6:30 asking who he is. If he is the Messiah why doesn't he perform a miracle for them as a sign? They throw up to him the thought that God gave their predecessors manna in the desert. "Give us this miracle too." They are sure their spirits will shrivel up and die if they let go of the pursuit of consumer goods and creature comforts. If God would perform a great miracle for them, they would believe. Give us proof, they plead. Do a great miracle and we will follow you.

Jesus responded to the crowd: "I am the bread of life. He who comes to me will never go hungry, and he who believes in me will never be thirsty." Certainly we need bread. We can't live without it. But Jesus uses a metaphor to show that we can't live by material possessions alone. We forget that the greater miracle than healing or something similar is always the working of the Spirit in the ordinary daily lives of children of God who trust him. And this symbol of bread dominates communion services together with the wine as a symbol of Christ's blood.

We need constant visible reminders that say to young and old, "Feed on me. Let my Spirit sustain you. I am the living bread. Let it become part of you and change your life so that you can move from despair to courage."

Columnist Dr. Laura Schlesinger writes about one young Jewish boy who was tempted to steal a toy at a pop-and-mom store. As he was about to take the item his hand brushed across his hair and touched his yarmulke, the cap Jews wear as a sign of respect to God. He ran out of the store without the toy. He realized he could not do something wrong and not have God know and be disappointed in him. The cap reminded him of his obligation to walk with God.

That is the point of all religious rituals and symbols, even hats, that our final obligation is to God. These concrete reminders will differ for different generations. In the Middle Ages, people were illiterate, so they learned the Bible stories as depicted in stained-glass windows. People today are computer literate but biblically illiterate. Is the time ripe to reintroduce stained-glass windows so children have something to puzzle through during services? For some the new symbols may be a stained-glass window, for others a wall motto, for still others a WWJD (What Would Jesus Do) bracelet.

The dangers of symbols

The symbol is not the reality. The use of symbols has dangers. They may lead people to think that the symbol can replace the reality. Symbols may convince people to believe that if they can say the words (symbols) of faith, they have the faith. A friend refers to this as memorized faith. I've known students to cheat to get an A—the symbol of a good grade.

When I was young, no serious Christians went anywhere without their "sword of the Lord" to turn to at any moment and to show others they were believers. This was commendable. But soon the larger the sword, the stronger symbol the Bible became of personal righteousness.

Deadness. Another danger of symbols is that the daily encounter with symbols can lead to deadness. People may turn the symbols into a kind of magic with protective powers. Missionary Anna B. Mow writes that one day in India she was called to visit a sick woman. Until her illness she had never read the Bible. However, she thought all that was necessary was to hold it in her hand. For her the Bible was magic only. She paid no attention to the living Word; she merely used the book as a charm (*Say Yes to Life*).

The ancient Jews wore a pair of small black boxes containing Scripture passages written on parchment on the upper left arm and above the forehead. This practice may have originated in response to Moses' words to the people to celebrate the feast of unleavened bread (Passover): "This observance will be for you like a sign on your hand and a reminder on your forehead that the law of the Lord is to be on your lips" (Exod. 13:9). At what point in their lives will children have begun asking the meaning of this small box?

Deuteronomy 6:8-9 instruct the Israelites to tie the parchments "as symbols on your hands and bind them on your foreheads. Write them on the doorframes of your houses and on your gates." Originally intended as a spiritual and educational device, the phylacteries' resemblance to amulets purported to offer protective powers. Therefore, certain people thought to be suscep-tible to demonic influence were forbidden to use them. In time, in Judaism, *mezuzah* was the term given to the container attached to the doorpost in which the Scripture passages were placed. For some, symbols of faith became empty body and door decorations.

In the New Testament Jesus speaks of the hypocritical Jewish leaders who flaunted the symbols of piety. They wore sackcloth, sprinkled ashes over their heads, went unbathed without anointing the head and body, and generally looked sad to show that they were fasting and thereby gain religious stature in the eyes of the people. Any adaptation of a manna jar, standing stone, or mezuzah can become empty when its sole purpose is to assure others that vital spiritual life dwells in the indi-vidual, family, or congregation.

Creativity adds to the symbolic process

The creative person aware of the power of symbols is a gift to the church. A worship committee of young and old might find challenging ways to make the commun-ion service more meaningful.

One morning at the college where I taught instead of

showy spring flowers in graceful vases, deadly weapons of war were scattered across the white cloth of the long communion table.

As we neared the table, the rifles, a gas mask, and shells starkly reminded us that we live in two kingdoms—the kingdom of God and the kingdom of this world. One is ruled by peace and love and the other by power, fear, and violence.

Partaking of the Lord's Supper can never mean exactly the same for every person. We do not need to fully understand to benefit from the observance, just as we don't need to understand the chemistry of food to be nourished by it.

Children grasp the significance of the symbolic, often better than adults who have the sense of wonder leached out of them. With the celebration of the Lord's Supper, we move into the area of the intangible, the symbolic, that which seems most fragile yet has overwhelming strength—strength greater than the mightiest weapon of war.

As I observed the weapons of war on that communion table, I wondered at the lives wasted by them. Then I looked at the true decorations on the Lord's table, the bread and wine, and marveled at lives made whole by the sacrifice of Christ's love. They were sitting all around me.

Symbols have value only when they direct people to the reality behind them. What was the reality behind the Last Supper Jesus had with his disciples? First they ate a regular meal together—somewhere in an upper room. Then the host rose to bless the bread. He took the loaf in his hands and broke it for them. This was the custom.

Then he did something new. He gave the loaf a name. He said, "This is my body." Then he gave the wine a name. He said, "This is my blood." Then he told the disciples to eat and drink in remembrance of him.

They were to remember that the cross would end Satan's control over their inner being. They were members of a new peaceable kingdom. God had established a new covenant with humanity. Christ's death and resurrection released an entirely new kind of power into the world—faith power—which makes whole and alive. It does not destroy.

The Lord's Supper reminds us symbolically that there is another way to decorate our lives. Our children need to see such reminders.

A manna jar for every family and congregation

Standing stones. Manna jars. Sounds like I'm promoting archaeological digs, doesn't it? Or more archival objects. That could be. Every family should have an archivist so that children learn to think of the family in terms of "we" instead of "I." Every congregation should have an archivist so that new and old members are aware that record keeping is important and that what they are enjoying in that church was built on the courage and sacrifice of those who came before them. And it helps if these archives aren't hidden in some locked closet and rarely displayed.

However, I am thinking of simpler things in home and sanctuary to keep reminding us of God's presence with us. Of course, every Christian is to be a "living stone" or "standing stone," a living testimony to the power and love of God, pointing to the God who is at work in our lives as he was in the world of the Israelites.

In the family the manna jar could be any clay or metal pot into which family members can drop a note about God's care. Each week the family would decide what they want to add to their jar. They could put into it some object to help them remember their own exodus from a life of selfish living to the life of Christ. They could add something that would jog their minds that God supplied their need during a wilderness wandering. They could put into the jar memories of the church growing stronger as a covenant body. But most important would be to keep showing these memories to children and grandchildren.

I have adopted the symbol of a windmill to represent my parents' spiritual and ethnic heritage. My father grew up on the steppes of the Ukraine in Russia where his father was a miller. Father learned the vagaries of the wind and internalized the words of Jesus about the Holy Spirit in John 3:8. He believed the Spirit could not be compelled to do human bidding. Every time I look at my pictures of his father's windmill, I remind myself of his belief in those words. Humans set up hoops for would-be seekers to jump through. The Holy Spirit "blows where it pleases."

Plan to erect symbolic standing stones or to place a symbolic manna jar in the

In my older friend's home hung a large framed wall motto in German of Joshua 24:15 painted on glass and backed by silver foil: "As for me and my household, we will serve the Lord." She told me its significance. Her grandparents chose this verse as their life motto. Both had become Christians in Russia. Before their marriage, her grandmother's father tempted them to reject their faith and stay in Russia with the promise of a large tract of land. They refused and determined even more to serve God. This wall motto reminded my friend not only of her grandparents' commitment but encouraged her to remain true to hers.

sanctuary, something people can point to again and again like the Israelites could point to the manna jar.

The younger generation doesn't have many experiences to draw upon, so it will have to be the task of the older generation to bring to their attention all the symbols of our corporate life as God's people. The elders will have to keep reminding the young what should be remembered as a family, and as a congregation. That may require reinventing symbols.

Now try this:

1. In one church I saw large framed pictures of the development of the church from a small one-room frame building to the present massive stone structure. How might such pictures give continuity to the church?

2. Is the WWJD (What Would Jesus Do?) bracelet a modern phylactery?

3. Though many congregations display wonderful wall banners, at the same time we have dropped the practice of hanging wall mottoes on home walls. Wall decorations, particularly those with religious themes, have proven to be important indicators of the processes of cultural transmission and change, writes Rolf Wilhelm Brednich in *Mennonite Folklore and Folklife*. Framed biblical texts were a compromise with the second commandment (not to make graven images) and yet have decorations on the walls. Such biblical texts were popular wedding gifts. Brednich traces the changes in these mottoes as well as the most popular religious pictures, still often seen, such as *Praying Hands, The Broad and the Narrow Way* by Charlotte Reihlen, *The Angelus*, and *Grace*. Should we encourage families to hang biblical texts in their homes?

4. What do you think of modern phylacteries such as rulers, pencils, pens, and T-shirts that have Scripture on them. Does that rob Scripture of its heroes?

5. What will remind children that they belong to the kingdom of God, not to the kingdom of this world? One Jewish father named his daughter the Hebrew equivalent of Elizabeth, not to separate her from America, but to separate her from what he perceived as the mainstream's lack of coherent morals and values. By giving her a traditional, biblical name, he hoped she would be reminded of the values that "used to be" and "ought to be" still. What difference does it make if parents give children names of Bible characters rather than modern celebrities?

6. At a women's conference, worshipers came forward during the service and lit a candle for some woman in their history whom they valued. Each candle stood for a remembered and honored life. It was a powerful reminder to me of the influence of women in the church.

Chapter 12

Touching the Future
Through Mentoring

*Most people who follow God's call come face-to-face,
consciously or unconsciously, with a person or an image
who embodies the concept of discipleship as they believe
it should be lived.*

Kelly, a college student, told me unabashedly she hadn't
done any studying last night. "Why not?" I asked.

"I watched *Little Women*."

"Why?"

"I liked it. I cried." I persisted in my questions. She
identified with Jo, the second oldest Marsh daughter of
Alcott's classic. Like Jo, she, too, wanted to write.

When I was in high school, I found myself wandering
through a fog. Then someone put a hand in mine and led
me through the confusion. The tomboyish, bookish Jo of
Alcott's *Little Women* whispered, "Go ahead, write. You
can do it." This irascible sister dared to be true to her
muse. She inspired me to be true to mine. And now
Kelly was telling me Jo was continuing to inspire another generation of young women.

Living in a small immigrant community in northern
Saskatchewan, Canada, made writing an impossible
dream. I knew no writers and writing was not held up as
an option to someone coming out of the Depression
years. You didn't make money writing. So I envied Jo.

Not until years later did I realize how much a real-life writing mentor-coach would have helped me.

Mentoring is needed to learn the skills of Christian discipleship as well as specific skills. Most people who follow God's call come face-to-face, consciously or unconsciously, with a person or an image who embodies the concept of discipleship as they believe it should be lived. That person becomes their inspiration. Another person did it. They can do it also. The younger person's willingness to be led by a mentor shouts his or her life goal to the world.

What is a mentor? The traditional meaning is a trusted counselor or guide. The word comes from ancient Greek mythology. Mentor became the loyal friend and adviser of the Greek hero Odysseus and the guardian and teacher of his son Telemachus. Erik H. Eriksen in *Childhood and Society* writes that mentors voluntarily commit themselves to guiding new generations and younger associates. In the Christian community it is a way of handing on the faith to new keepers. It is a way of touching the future.

A mentor may be a parent, friend, relative, teacher; but also a character in a novel or biography, or a public figure like a political or religious leader. My first mentor was a purely symbolic fictional figure, which is true for many aspiring writers. That person's spirit draws them forward. I never found a real-life writing mentor, but later I often turned to published writers like A. W. Tozer and Elton Trueblood whose ideas, style, and forthrightness I admired. I hesitate to place celebrities and athletes in this mentor category although it is possible that some might draw the best out of a young person, especially a coach during a child's formative years.

The task of a mentor varies. A mentor is a combination of teacher, counselor, sponsor, guide, and model. Primarily, the older person oversees the development of the younger man or woman in one or more areas of life for a time, not often for extended years.

A mentor is a transitional figure who cuts away the underbrush during crucial periods in the younger person's life and makes room for him or her to move forward. The mentor helps Jane or George shape her or his vision for life and encourages the young person to reach for the stars. Mentors help younger persons to have confidence in their own judgment, abilities, and gifts. They help them sort through problems and plan strategies to solve them.

One of the "promises" to every child of "America's Promise: The Alliance for Youth," a national organization whose director is General Colin Powell, is an ongoing relationship with an adult who can be a parent, mentor, tutor, or coach. This recently organized group has as its goal to mobilize individuals, groups, and organizations from every part of American life to build and strengthen the character and competence of all the nation's young people. The way to do it is by getting up close and personal.

Mentors help the inexperienced youth to withstand group and societal pressures to conform to their values; for example, not to tolerate false images of femininity or masculinity. They model an integrated attitude toward work, play, career, and relationships. Mentors encourage the younger person to risk, because of the possibilities for personal growth and service, not because of the guarantee that will happen.

Above all, a mentor is a trusted voice of authority who says, "You can do it—keep moving! I've been over this way. I know where some of the hurdles are. Use me as your model." Students used to tell me that they never really believed their essay was worth an A until I wrote A on it. In the same way a mentor writes a big A for "you can do it" over a younger person's life.

Paul wrote in his first letter to the Thessalonian church (1:5-7) that just as he had been their model or mentor they were to mentor others: "You know how we lived among you for your sake. You became imitators of us and of the Lord. . . . And so you became a model to all the believers in Macedonia and Achaia." He was giving them a big A for living out their faith in Christ after the model he gave when it was an unusual way to live.

Servant ministry. Mentoring is a type of servant ministry with the older person letting go of power in order to make more room for the younger one. The process of mentoring breaks down when one generation refuses to let go of its roles and responsibilities and the next generations must beg, plead, or grab for opportunity.

In Bunyan's Pilgrim's Progress, toward the end of their journey, Christian and his traveling companion Hopeful reach the river they must cross before they arrive at the Celestial City. Hopeful enters the water first and Christian follows. But at once he is certain he is drowning and cries out: "I sink in deep waters; the billows go over my head, all his waves go over me!" Hopeful calls out to him, "Brother, be of good cheer. I feel the bottom and it is firm."

Life is not easy. Life is not fair. Younger generations need those who have entered the waters before them to cry out, "Be of good cheer. We feel the bottom and it is firm."

Canadian churchman Henry J. Gerbrandt writes in his memoirs of a time when the mentoring process broke down between him and an older church leader. He admired Bishop Schulz of the Bergthaler Mennonite Church. He enjoyed his sermons and turned to him for counsel at key times in his life. The older Schulz guided the younger Gerbrandt in many areas of church life. But as Schulz became older, he found giving up power difficult. Tensions arose about language, youth work, and constitutional changes. Traditions that had carried the church since 1837 were breaking down.

The time came for Gerbrandt to take over Schulz's position in the church. In 1962, at Gerbrandt's installation service as leading minister of the Altona Church in Manitoba, he was to give a tribute to the older man's years of contribution to the church.

(continued)

Mentoring can lead to a stronger sense of peoplehood as the younger person is introduced to church ministry. In the process of making room for him or her to develop and exercise gifts of the Spirit, self-indulgence on the part of the older person must give way to a spirit of generosity, and the Spirit of Christ has opportunity to lead.

Benefits of mentoring. The benefits of mentors extend in several directions. The younger generation is well served when a community includes a range of mature and generative adults, write Evelyn Eaton Whitehead and James D. Whitehead in *Christian Life Patterns*. Some young people may not want an older person interfering in their lives, yet the benefit of a mentor always gives the individual a head start in life, they state.

On the other hand, the older person who voluntarily nurtures younger men and women will find the experience enriching and freeing. Giving up power with dignity and deliberately transferring it to the next generation is renewing for the middle-aged or older person. It is a way of reproducing oneself, of generating one's life, and finding freedom from self-indulgence. And the thread of continuity between the generations remains unbroken.

Who needs a mentor?

Boys and men need mentors. The role of mentor used to be restricted to the business, academic, and professional world, particularly to young men, for they were expected to push ahead into new areas of thought and leadership. Young men were coached and groomed for a higher position.

Girls and women need mentors also. Decades ago women had mentors too, but they weren't usually considered formal mentors, for they were mothers, aunts, friends, and grandmothers. Young wives and mothers were guided or encouraged by an older woman through the crises of early homemaking and child-caring.

In 1970, a generation ago, sociologist Helen Lopata conducted a study of 571 women. She asked them: "Where have you gotten help in learning to perform your homemaker role? How did you learn to do this task

Schulz, on the other hand, was to preach the installation service for Gerbrandt. It didn't turn out that way.

After Gerbrandt's words of affirmation of the older man's ministry, Schulz rose to speak. In his address Schulz never mentioned Gerbrandt or referred to any kind of installation. After he sat down the congregation was very silent. Then Mrs. Schulz got up and said, "You don't know how hard it is for my husband to do what he was asked to do. He could not do it." On her husband's behalf she wished Mr. and Mrs. Gerbrandt God's blessing in their ministry.
—En Route: The Memoirs of Henry J. Gerbrandt

When my husband began his pastoral ministry in the 1950s, his mentor was a retired pastor, short in stature but big in heart. When he came calling at the door, with a twinkle in his eye, he always asked if his "big brother" was in. Walter was six feet two inches. He regularly spent many hours with Walter in his study yet stimulated freedom in ministry. The older man said he found fulfillment in seeing the inexperienced pastor develop under his guidance. My husband mentioned he felt more secure knowing he had someone behind him to lean on when congregational problems got rough.

creatively and competently?" The majority of respondents did not list older generation members. They listed courses, books, magazines, newspapers, radio and TV. Only 35 percent referred to "mother," 9 percent to "home," and 4 percent to other relatives.

Today, that mentoring function has been taken over even more by the media which offer advice and encouragement on every aspect of home living with Martha Stewart as the good homemaker guru. The number of publications and programs for beautifying and improving homes and gardens has proliferated. But something is missing—the personal relationship or the influence of one life on another through intimate contact.

Young mothers, especially those separated from their own mothers, by time and distance, need the wisdom and steadiness of older women assuring them of God's grace for the trying problems of family living. One older woman with whom I had contact for about a decade birthed her seventh child when my first daughter was born.

Our beds stood side by side in a crowded 15-bed hospital maternity ward just after World War II, so I had opportunity to observe her well. Her sense of creative partnership with God as a mother rubbed off on me. I watched the way she lovingly dealt with her large family then and later in our church community.

Mentors are needed in church life. Mentors are needed for young women moving into the uncharted territory of church life and service. An older generation is needed to recognize and affirm the spiritual gifts of women for new roles, to nominate them for positions, and then make living space for them on boards, committees, and in conversation during coffee breaks in congregations where women's ministry is still an issue.

They are also needed to guide both men and women into pastoral work at a time when this role is no longer sought as highly. Earlier in this book, results from The Samuel Project, a study by the Mennonite Church (USA and Canada) to tell the church community why and how youth respond to the call of God and the church to serve as pastors, showed that Mennonite youth do not flock to church vocations because of a lack of specific encouragement. Encouragement is not intentional. Years ago this was referred to as "tap on the shoulder" of the younger man by an older man. Today it is needed for both men and women.

The Samuel Report states clearly that "there is strong evidence that respondents who have been personally encouraged to consider the ministry are more likely to say that they have a 'calling' and more likely to have considered preparing for the ministry."

Adults need mentors. Writer Naomi Gaede-Penner calls for mentors for adults, not just for children and young people. She calls this "uncharted territory." Singles/widows/single parents are just a few of the examples she cites of people needing mentors. When I was newly widowed I yearned to have an older widow show me the way through this unstable territory I didn't want to traverse.

Young parents, especially those separated from their own families because of geographic distance and single parents, need the wisdom and steadiness of older men and women assuring them of God's grace for the most trying problems of family living. Yet our closely graded Sunday schools, especially in large congregations, make it almost impossible for different generations to become close friends.

The creative young person needs a mentor. The developing writer, poet, or artist needs an affirmer of gifts not always readily accepted by the broader church body. The presence or absence of such a role model, mentor, or hero has an enormous impact on the development of the one who is testing the unknown limits of creativity. The truly creative person often scares people in the church by moving outside the accepted structures. A mentor can encourage creative persons to know their gift, speak openly about it, and commit themselves to using it to extend the kingdom of God. To find your gift means you hold yourself responsible before God for all that you are.

Retirees need a mentor. Another category where mentors are needed is those adults making the transition into a new life after completing their work careers. When I was getting ready to quit teaching I wanted to talk about aging with those who had traveled this path ahead of me. No one wanted to talk about growing older. Old, of course, was a taboo word. "It's too frightening to talk about," said one. "Aging is a tough proposition," came from another. No one invited me to grow old along with them.

When I turned to books on aging and retirement I found that many of them had been written by young professionals who had all kinds of theoretical action plans for successful aging. They suggested how to make finances last, how to look after health, how to find the best housing, how to untangle legal affairs. Too few were written by people who knew that suddenly to find you are not immune to arthritis or other ills is like a slap in the face, that gray hair equals incompetence in the minds of some people, that the lions of the later years crouch close to your door if you are not watchful. I wanted to know where my older friends found grace and spiritual strength for living. I have since found that other elders are looking for spiritual mentors as they enter the afternoon of life.

What does it take to be a mentor?

Biblical examples. Mentoring is a biblical concept. Consider the examples of the great prophet Elijah who tutored his student Elisha and at the end left him his mantle and his prophetic commission (1 Kings 19).

The veteran missionary Paul counseled his untested worker Timothy (1, 2 Timothy).

Naomi gave her widowed daughter-in-law Ruth advice when her kinsman Boaz showed a marrying interest in her (Ruth).

Elizabeth, older cousin to Mary, encouraged the younger woman during her perplexing pregnancy (Luke 1).

The priest Eli counseled the young boy Samuel when he came to the older man perplexed about how to respond to God's call (1 Samuel 3). In each case there was a close relationship between mentor and mentee.

Gaede-Penner sees this close relationship as most important for the young to develop an interest in missions. She states that older generations support mission organizations out of what could be termed "obedience to Christ" and the "right thing to do." The new generation supports missions where there have been prior friendships or where there is the opportunity for such to evolve.

She writes in *The Christian Leader* that one generation is satisfied to display missionary prayer cards on the refrigerator door or to add another colored tack to the missionary map to remind them to pray. A young generation insists on knowing the missionaries if they are expected to support them. Mentoring works best when mentor and mentee know one another and aren't just "secret pals" who pray for one another and send cards at birthdays and Christmas.

Younger generations follow into missionary service when they have models close at hand. The Mennonite church has many families where two or three generations have worked in missions. The P. A. Friesen family has four generations who have served the church in mission through the Mennonite Board of Missions. Jonathan Friesen, the newest Friesen in mission, writes in *Mennonite Weekly Review*: "Generations of Friesens have gone a long way from home. They have been instrumental to me in having me live out my faith. . . . They taught me through their actions."

The Mennonite Brethren D. F. Bergthold family also has four generations that have served in India and other places. Nearly every branch of the church can point to families with strong service traditions modeled by the previous generations. Close contact seems to be the key.

New Testament mentoring. An often cited New Testament passage is Titus 2:3-5, especially the phrase "keepers at home" (KJV). It has been used to cudgel women into accepting a role as stay-at-home moms. I see it differently. The apostle Paul was writing to a church emerging from paganism. Christ-believing women needed to be taught the behavior accompanying faith early in their married life. Faith without the works of a righteous life was dead. They needed a mentor to guide them over unfamiliar territory of how to be a Christian wife.

In his letter to Timothy, Paul told the younger man to urge older women to exercise some of the same graces as was expected of an overseer (1 Tim. 3). Titus was to teach the older women to be "reverent in the way they live, not to be slanderers or addicted to much wine" (Titus 2:3). They, in turn, were to teach younger women what is good. In Titus he is concerned that a young wife be a husband-lover and a children-lover. They were to be self-controlled and pure, to be busy at home (to be good managers of the household, NRSV), to be kind, and to be submissive to their husbands, so that no one would malign the word of God (Titus 2:3-5).

Working outside the home was not an option for women in biblical times. Paul knew that, to a great extent, the world would judge the Christian faith by the quality of family life and what it did for women. He gave older women a moral choice just like he gave men a moral choice—to mentor younger women. What higher commission could one receive?

One woman who had been over the path was expected to reach back and intentionally help the younger one find the way and stay on it. Recipes for zucchini bread or make-ahead party potatoes were not as important as how to love children and husband, and how to face life head on with joy, courage, and faith. Such teaching of younger women by older women is especially important at a time when the glue of family is drying out.

What traits does a mentor have? Mentors may not always have great academic knowledge in psychology and the sciences but they do have the skills of living and through consistent close encounters they can pass these on. Grandparents can mentor all age-groups. Adults can mentor young people. High school students can mentor grade school students.

A loving relationship. Educators agree that a key element in mentoring is frequent long-term contact and a warm, loving relationship in a variety of life settings in which the mentor exhibits consistent behavior and values. The best format is a regular, natural exchange of values and experiences regardless of age.

A child development expert told a public gathering here in Wichita this spring that today's society was the "most child-unfriendly society he knew of, the most age-segregated society that has ever existed in the history of human civilization." He said: "We have forgotten our own power, as human beings . . . to affect the lives of children." He asserted that forming relationships with young people—talking to them, appreciating them, encouraging them, getting to know them—does make a difference.

Vulnerability. Mentors make themselves vulnerable by freely exposing their inner lives, and where there is a comfortable fit, sharing the spiritual disciplines of prayer and Bible study. Can they honestly say they have a regular devotional period? What is the role of prayer in their lives? How did they learn to forgive? To be patient?

To resist the temptation to smoke? To give up smoking? To sleep with girl or boyfriend? How did the mentors overcome the hurts caused by family wounds? What values have they discarded over time and why? Which have they kept? Does their theology, whatever it may be, work in real life, not just on paper in beautifully worded statements? If so, where? What tasks are still incomplete, like forgiveness of a parent or sibling?

This transparency in relationship may take a while to develop, but it bonds the two together more closely. Sociologist Dwight Roth writes that for 20 years he has had students in his Helping Relationship class at Hesston College. Each student spends one hour a week visiting with elders in the community in a grandparent adoption program. "These relationships usually prove to be very powerful for participants," he writes. "The elders and young people seem almost magnetically drawn to each other." On occasion when Hesston College alumni return to campus they visit the elder who 10, 15, or even 20 years ago was their adopted grandparent while they were a student at the college.

Clear vision. Mentees need reassurance, comfort, and support to give them a sense of stability and courage to move ahead. But they also need an older person to encourage their vision of the young person's potential.

A mentor or sponsor helps a younger person, whether a boomer or Generation Xer, to withstand societal pressures to become a cookie cutter replica of what society upholds as the ideal person instead of developing his or her own gifts and talents. Gaede-Penner of Denver claims an aunt and uncle as her mentors. Why? "They have a life of their own, they are self-giving, they are curious, they are alive, they have a sense of humor. I want to be like them."

My son in middle school years had a series of college students as his Big Brothers for several years through a social work program. His father had died when he was nearly four. They provided masculine activities, talk, and viewpoints. For several years weekend campouts were a regular feature. College students Paul and Harley packed up a group of young boys and their sleeping bags for an overnight at the nearby reservoir. Systematic mother-type packing may have been missing, but the boys enjoyed their outings even when snow frosted their sleeping bags or the fried eggs stuck to the pan at breakfast because butter was missing.

Equally exciting to James were opportunities to spend a night in the men's dormitory at the college and go out for pizza at midnight. James reported one day that some boys with fathers were jealous of his Big Brother, who involved

(continued)

Role models of the faith. Mentors are role models of faith in Christ, not perfect people, but those who show by life and word that they are on a pilgrimage of faith, and are ready to keep learning. Mentors say to the younger person, "There is a spirit needed in society other than the selfish one that dominates. It is the spirit of caring and reaching for long-range goals rather than short-term satisfaction."

The daily newspaper cites dozens of examples of mentoring taking place in the broader city community. A high school student was mentoring an elementary school student with his schoolwork. A community woman was honored for donating her time to tutor children in one of the lower economic areas of the city in a local church and bringing snacks for them for three years.

A friend, Fred Haney, who began an early television station in Wichita and continues an interest in electronics and carpentry, volunteered to help with set construction for the drama class at North High School. One high school student had never operated any kind of power tools, so he taught her to drive screws into drywall with a power drill. She was able to attach the drywall for the set onto the frame. Later, at a cast party, she told him, "I had a good day with my father today because I had learned to drill screws." His mentoring helped her in her relationship with her father. Fred told me he never knew he had done anything special for her. Later on, the cast celebrated his birthday with a cake, surprising him.

Roth cites Urie Bronfenbrenner who wrote in 1970 that the "phenomenon of segregation by age and its consequences for human behavior and development pose prob-

him in so much fun. It seemed a strange reversal of roles to him. "When I have something on my mind, I can go talk it over with Tim," James once explained. God and girls, flying and computers, school and sisters. All needed a sounding board.

When James heard that Harley was leaving for voluntary service after graduation from college, his eyes filled with tears. I was sorry with him. Harley had been a special friend to him.
—Alone, a Widow's Search for Joy. Used by permission of Kindred Press.

lems of the greatest magnitude for the Western world in general and for the American society in particular."

Bronfenbrenner concludes that "if the current trend persists [and it has], if the institutions of our society continue to remove parents, other adults, and older youth from active participation in the lives of children [and who will not admit that they do], and if the resulting vacuum is filled by the age segregated peer groups, we can anticipate increased alienation, indifference, antagonism, violence on the part of the younger generation in all segments of our society—middle-class children as

In one congregation each baptismal candidate is assigned a lay adult mentor for both fellowship and spiritual direction. Mentors attend the catechism classes with the candidates and are encouraged to include these young people when they are engaged in church responsibilities, such as mission meetings. "This bridges a connection between those who are well established in the faith and those who need to be nurtured in it, the goal being to encourage young people to lay claim to their own gifts," said one leader. "The process is expected to develop an adult member of the faith, who knows the language and rituals of faith, and has seen firsthand the life of a believer."
—Christianity Today, "The Class of '00," by Wendy Murray Zoba, February 3, 1997

well as the disadvantaged." These are words to heed.

Now try this:

1. Dwight E. Roth of Hesston College, Hesston, Kansas, thinks he has discovered a way for an older generation to help younger people meet the challenges of the present. He has developed what he calls the HOME (Hesston Online Mentoring and Education) program. This unique program connects Hesston College students via e-mail with individuals throughout the United States and the world. Mentors and teachers are Hesston College alumni and/or older adults—anyone 50 years of age or older who has interest in interacting in a positive, generative way with younger people.

   HOME is just one of several programs Roth has developed to bring the energy and heroism of youth and the wisdom and generativity of older people together. He admits that this connection generally needs to be structured—intentionally and strategically.

2. Big Brother/Big Sister programs are huge assists to boys and girls who may have only one parent for various reasons.

3. "GrandFriends" matches older adults from the congregation with children to build a friendship between the generations. Each child chooses an older member of the congregation to be their special GrandFriend. The child and older person exchange cards and personal information about themselves. Early in the school year the pairs attend a church service together so they can meet face-to-face. In addition they pray for one another. Children are encouraged to ask their GrandFriend for specific information, say, like about the Great Depression or personal experiences.

4. In researching this book I found that some congregations have an "Every Student with a Shepherd" program with training programs for the adult volunteers, especially effective for young people who don't have significant adults in their lives. But the problem comes up to find time for other people's kids, let alone one's own.

5. Phone Pals is a program designed to help students when they are alone before or after school. The older adult calls the student every day either before or after school and sometimes both times. Parents, children, and phone pals and other family members get together three times a year for parties. This is similar to a foster grandparent program.

6. Midweek church suppers offer excellent opportunities for young and old to mingle at the table. Last night I attended a Lorraine Avenue Mennonite Church supper. Across from me sat the young youth

director and his fiancée. At the same table were several boomers as well as another older woman. Church suppers are a good setting for intergenerational interaction, I told myself, if those who attend don't clump automatically into age-groupings.

7. Study each of the biblical examples of mentoring mentioned in this chapter. What do they all have in common? What is unique about each example?

Bibliography

Anderson, Bernhard W. and Stephen Bishop. *Out of the Depths: The Psalms Speak for Us Today.* Louisville, Ky.: Westminister John Knox Press, 2000.

Barna, George. *Generation Next: What You Need to Know About Today's Youth.* Ventura, Calif.: Regal Books, 1997.

Brueggeman, Walter. *The Prophetic Imagination.* Philadelphia: Fortress Press, 1978.

———— *The Land: Place as Gift, Promise, and Challenge in Biblical Faith.* Philadelphia: Fortress Press, 1977.

Chinen, Allen B. *The Ever After: Fairy Tales and the Second Half of Life.* Wilmette, Ill.: Chiron, 1997.

Driver, John. *Becoming God's Community:* The Foundation Series. Scottdale, Pa.: Herald Press, 1981.

———— *Community and Commitment.* Scottdale, Pa.: Herald Press, 1976.

———— *Images of the Church in Mission.* Scottdale, Pa.: Herald Press, 1997.

Dychtwald, Ken. *Age Power.* New York: J. P. Tarcher, 1999.

Dychtwald, Ken and Joe Flower. *Age Wave: How the Most Important Trend of Our Time Will Change Your Future.* New York: Bantam Books, 1990.

Elshtain, Jean Bethke. "Review of *She Said Yes: The Unlikely Martyrdom of Cassie Bernall* by Misty Bernall." *The New Republic,* January 17, 2000.

Ekerst, David J. "The Busy Ethic."*Generations, Journal of the American Society of Aging,* Fall 1996.

Eriksen, Erik. *Childhood and Society.* New York: W. W. Norton & Company, 1993.

Eriksen, Erik, et al. *Vital Involvement in Old Age.* New York: W. W. Norton & Company, 1986.

Gentzler, Richard H., Jr. and Donald F. Clingan. *Aging: God's Challenge to Church and Synagogue.* Nashville, Tenn.: Discipleship Resources, 1996.

Gerbrandt, Gerald. "The 21st Century Calling for a Faithful Community—Strategies," *What Mennonites Are Thinking.* Edited by Merle Good and Phyllis Pellman Good. Intercourse, Pa.: Good Books, 1999.

Gerbrandt, Henry J. *En Route: The Memoirs of Henry J. Gerbrandt.* Winnipeg, Man.: CMBC Publications, 1994.

Greenleaf, Robert K. *Servant Leadership: A Journey into the Nature of Legitimate Power and Greatness.* New York: Paulist Press, 1977.

Harder, Bertha, editor. *Young or Old or In Between: An Intergenerational Study on Aging, Reader and Leader's Guide.* Newton, Kan.: Faith & Life Press, 1986.

Hershberger, Anne Krabill, editor. *Sexuality: God's Gift.* Scottdale, Pa.: Herald Press, 1999.

Hillman, James. *The Force of Character and the Lasting Life.* New York: Ballantine Books, 1999.

Hudson, Frederic M. *The Adult Years: Mastering the Art of Self-Renewal.* San Francisco: Jossey Bass, 1991.

Kavanaugh, John. *Following Christ in a Consumer World.* Maryknoll, New York: Orbis Books, 1991.

Kivnick, Helen Q. "Remembering and Being Remembered." *Generations, Journal of the American Society on Aging,* Fall 1996.

Kobelt-Groch, Marion. "'Hear my son the instructions of your mother': Children and Anabaptism," The EnGendering the Past Symposium, *Journal of Mennonite Studies*, Vol. 17, 1999.

Konrad, George. *Living as God's Family*: Foundation Series. Scottdale, Pa.: Herald Press, 1981.

Krahn, Cornelius. *The Witness of the Martyr's [sic] Mirror for Our Day.* North Newton, Kan.: Bethel College, n.d.

Leinwand, Gerald. *Heroism in America.* New York: Franklin Watts, 1996.

Maloney, H. Newton. "The Graying of America." *Christianity Today,* January 17, 1996.

Marstin, Ronald. *Beyond Our Tribal Gods: The Maturing of Faith.* Maryknoll, New York: Orbis, 1979.

McElroy, Brenda Heinrichs. "Fig Garden Bible Church on the Move," *The Christian Leader,* October 1999.

Mouw, Richard. *Uncommon Decency.* Downers Grove, Ill.: InterVarsity Press, 1992.

Pipher, Mary. *Another Country: Navigating the Emotional Terrain of Our Elders.* New York: Penguin/Putnam, 1999.

Roth, Dwight. *Aging and Modernization: Among the Yoder Amish and Hesston Mennonites,* M.A. Thesis. 1981.

Schachter-Shalomi, Zalman and Ronald S. Miller. *From AGE-ing to SAGE-ing.* New York: Warner, 1995.

Sinetar, Marsha. *The Mentor's Spirit.* New York: St. Martin's Press, 1998.

Showalter, Shirley Hershey. "Two Stories on a Continuing Journey," in *She Has Done a Good Thing: Mennonite Women Tell Their Stories,* Mary Swartley and Rhoda Keener, editors. Scottdale, Pa.: Herald Press, 1999.

Snyder, C. Arnold and Linda A. Huebert Hecht, editors. *Profiles of Anabaptist Women: Sixteenth Century Reforming Pioneers.* Waterloo, Ont.: Wilfrid Laurier University Press, 1996.

Tobin, Sheldon S. "Cherished Possessions: The Meaning of Things." *Generations, Journal of the American Society on Aging,* Fall 1996.

Tournier, Paul. *The Seasons of Life.* Richmond, Va.: John Knox Press, 1963.

Van Braght, Thieleman J. *Martyrs Mirror: The Story of Seventy Centuries of Christian Martyrdom.* Scottdale, Pa.: Herald Press, 1997.

Whitehead, Evelyn Eaton, and James D. Whitehead. *Christian Life Patterns: The Psychological Challenges and Religious Invitations of Adult Life.* New York: Doubleday, 1979

Wiens, Delbert. "From the Village to the City," *DIRECTION,* Vol. II, October/73 & January/74.

Winner, Lauren F. "Sword Drills and Stained Glass: What children really learn in Sunday school." *Christianity Today,* April 5, 1999.

Wuthnow Robert. *After Heaven: Spirituality in America Since the 1950s.* Berkley, Calif.: University of California Press, 1998.

———— *Growing Up Religious: Christians and Jews and Their Journeys of Faith.* Boston: Beacon Press, 1999.

———— *The Struggle for America's Soul: Evangelicals, Liberals, and Secularism.* Grand Rapids, Mich.: William B. Eerdmans, 1989.

Zoba, Wendy Murray. "The Class of '00," *Christianity Today.* Feb. 3, 1997.

The Author

Katie Funk Wiebe is professor emerita of Tabor College, Hillsboro, Kansas, where she taught English for 24 years. She has written hundreds of articles and authored or edited 16 books including *Bless Me Too, My Father*, which won the Silver Angel award, and *Border Crossing: A Spiritual Journey*.

Wiebe grew up in northern Saskatchewan, the daughter of Russian-German immigrants. She now lives in Wichita, Kansas, where she is a member of the First Mennonite Brethren Church. She is the mother for three children and grandmother of six.